Ramesh S. Balsekar is known and loved by seekers from around the world as an eloquent Master of Advaita, or non-duality. After retiring as President of the Bank of India, Ramesh translated many of the daily talks given in Marathi by his Guru Nisargadatta Maharaj. The teaching began in 1982 after Maharaj had twice directed him to talk, and since then he has written over twenty books on Advaita.

By the Same Author

The Ultimate Understanding (2002)
Advaita, the Buddha and the Unbroken Whole (2000)
Sin and Guilt: Monstrosity of Mind (2000)
Meaningful Trivialities from the Source (2000)
The Infamous Ego (1999)
Who Cares? (1999)
The Essence of the Bhagavad Gita (1999)
Your Head in the Tiger's Mouth (1998)
Consciousness Writes (1996)
A Net of Jewels (1996)
The Bhagavad Gita – A Selection (1995)
Like a Large Immovable Rock (1994)
Ripples (1994)
Consciousness Speaks (1992)
From Consciousness to Consciousness (1989)
The Final Truth (1989)
The Duet of One (1989)
Experiencing the Teaching (1988)
Explorations into The Eternal (1987)
Experience of Immortality (1987)

IT SO HAPPENED THAT...

The Unique Teaching of
Ramesh S. Balsekar

Watkins Publishing
London

This edition published in the UK in 2003 by
Watkins Publishing, 20 Bloomsbury Street, London, WC1B 3QA

© Ramesh S. Balsekar 2003

Rameseh S Balsekar has asserted his right under the Copyright, Designs and Patents Act, 1988, to be identified as author of this work.

All rights reserved.

No part of this book may be reproduced or utilized in any form or by any means, electronic or mechanical, without prior permission in writing from the Publishers.

Cover design by Echelon Design
Cover photograph from the author
Designed and typeset by Jerry Goldie
Printed and bound in Great Britain

British Library Cataloguing in Publication data available

Library of Congress Cataloging in Publication data available

ISBN 1 84293 064 8

www.watkinspublishing.com

CONTENTS

INTRODUCTION	VII
THE BASICS	1
CONSCIOUSNESS	8
NO PERSONAL DOER, NO INDIVIDUAL 'ME'	15
FREE WILL	17
THE 'ME' OR THE EGO	28
THE THINKING MIND AND THE WORKING MIND	32
WITNESSING	34
CHILDREN AND THEIR UNDERSTANDING	38
CONCEPTS	40
INTERRELATED OPPOSITES	41
INTERRELATED OPPOSITES – PAIN, SUFFERING AND EVIL	44
INTERRELATED OPPOSITES – DEATH	46
ACCEPTANCE AND SURRENDER	52
SEEKING	57
SELF-INQUIRY	66
SADHANA	68
SADHANA – PRAYER	77
SADHANA – ASCETICISM AND DENIAL	79
SADHANA – RITUAL	82
THE GURU – DISCIPLE RELATIONSHIP	83
BHAKTI AND JNANA	86
AWAKENING	90
A SAGE'S REALITY	93
PERSONAL STORIES ABOUT RAMESH	103

INTRODUCTION

Ramesh Balsekar always speaks about the same subject, Consciousness, but never in quite the same way. His talks are spontaneous and he welcomes, almost requires, questions from his listeners. (He humorously threatens to read from his extensive collection of written material if no questions are forthcoming. This threat can be quite effective.)

Ramesh's personality has a love for stories, an excellent and encompassing sense of humor, spontaneity, and a sense of comic timing that often has people laughing at their own struggles, and at the nature of the predicament that they are in as seekers. For example, at one seminar after he had given a brief introduction, Ramesh said, 'So what is the first question? But before that... the moment that I said that it reminded me of a joke. A rabbi was besieged with people seeing him from morning until evening so he had no time for himself to read or to contemplate or to meditate. He didn't know what to do, and then it struck him. So he put up a notice on his board: "One hundred dollars for two questions." Now, of course, he had plenty of free time during the day. Then one rich man came and he said, "Rabbi, here is a hundred dollars. Isn't a hundred dollars for two questions too much?" The rabbi said, "Yes. What is your next question?"'

Since 1987 Ramesh has given talks and seminars in the United States, Germany, and South India. He is also available to visitors in his home most mornings of the year, and people drop by when they are in Bombay to attend those gatherings. If you have been bitten by the Advaitic bug, as I have, and you find yourself attending many of his talks, you will hear the same stories, anecdotes, quotes from other sources, and jokes again and again as Ramesh illustrates the basic concepts that make up the Advaitic teachings. I have never tired of these illustrations. In fact, they have become measures of the deepening of my understanding from one seminar to the next. And, like the thread that holds together the beads on a necklace, these illustrations string in place for me the often slippery and elusive concepts of the teaching.

Last year in Germany I told Ramesh I would like to collect his stories in a book. He welcomed the idea as he seems to welcome most of his followers' creative ventures. (I suspect that is because he understands that the writing will benefit the writer in his or her understanding, perhaps more than it will be of help to the readers!) I have learned that when creative ideas appear with any force and persistence in my mind, they should be pursued. So with Ramesh's blessings I began this project that day by sitting around a table with him, Wayne Liquorman, Marc Beuret, and Heiner Siegelmann recalling stories and by taping Ramesh recounting some of his favorites. The stories that I collected that day started off this project. The rest were gleaned from tapes of his seminars in Kovalam Beach, India, in Tiburon, Seattle, Aspen, and Maui in the U.S.A., and in Gut Schermau, Germany.

The format I have chosen is to lightly edit an introductory talk that Ramesh gave at one of the Gut Schermau seminars in 1999. This talk lays out Ramesh's basic concepts, followed by further concepts and illustrations that he often uses in his talks and in answering questions. The stories, jokes, quotes and anecdotes are assembled with a minimum of editorial explanation, under subject headings. In this way, this book can be read from cover to cover, or used as a reference.

Ramesh's talks are sprinkled with quotes and passages from, and stories about, books that he has read. 'I have never really gone and sought a book, but it's been my experience that books have a mysterious way of coming into my hands. Earlier I used to say, "I'm not interested." But at a certain point I stopped rejecting any book. Any book that came I would go through, and more often than not that book had a certain significance.' He says that the reason for so many stories about rabbis is that his friends, Norton and Albe

Smith, gave him an excellent book called *The Rabbi Stories*. He also says that he never knows when he will tell a story. They just appear spontaneously as he speaks.

As Ramesh teaches, it is very easy to see both the personality of the body-mind organism that is Ramesh, and Consciousness working through that personality that It has created.

Mary Ciofalo
San Francisco, California
2000

THE BASICS

'One of the first things I tell each group is this: Whatever I say is a concept. It is not the truth. I say this in the beginning because I daresay what I say will appeal to you, and within five or ten seconds your mind will say, "This appeals to me. But how do I know it's the truth?" So I'll tell you right at the beginning, it's not the truth! It's only a concept. What do I mean by a concept? A concept is something which some people may accept and some people will deny. The other thing about a concept is that it can be interpreted in two or more ways. Let me give you an example:

> A king dreamt that all his teeth had fallen out. He called for the court astrologer. The court astrologer interpreted the dream, saying, 'Your Majesty, this is a very bad dream. This says all your relatives will die.' So the king was angry and sent him to prison. Then he sent for another astrologer. This astrologer, knowing what had happened to the first one, said, 'Majesty, this is a very good omen. This says that you will outlive all your relatives.' The king rewarded this astrologer.

'So, the same concept can be interpreted in two ways. About this there is also a joke:

> A man had the habit of saying, 'It could have been worse.' Every time something happened, almost certainly he would say, 'It could have been worse.' One morning a friend came and said to the man, 'Do you know what happened last night? Fred went home unexpectedly, found his wife in bed with a friend, and he shot them both and now Fred is in jail.' So this man said, 'Oh, that's very bad. Most unfortunate.' Then he added, 'It could have been worse.' The friend got angry

at this reply. He said, 'What do you mean? One friend is in jail, his wife and another person are dead! How could it have been worse?' The man replied, 'Well, it's this way. This happened last night. If it had happened the previous night, I would have been dead.'

'A concept is something which can be interpreted. Therefore I say, whatever I say is a concept; it is not the Truth. Is there something which is the Truth, which goes beyond interpretation? Yes, there is. There is a Truth which no one can deny, and that is the impersonal awareness of existence, "I am. I exist." That impersonal awareness of existence is in every human being; no one will deny that he exists. An atheist may deny that God exists, but he cannot deny that he exists. This impersonal awareness of existence, "I am," is the only Truth. And that Truth prevails in phenomenality, in life as we know it. The Source is not concerned with Truth, the Source is the Truth. When a spiritual seeker wants to know the Truth, he assumes that It must be beyond life or prior to life, and therefore the misconception often is that the spiritual seeking must transcend life. My concept is exactly the other way around. Any spiritual concept which does not refer to life as we know it will not be much good. *So my first concept "I Am" is the only Truth, and "I Am" is life as we know it, or the functioning of manifestation.*

'*The second basic concept* is that the human being is just one species of objects along with thousands of species of objects in land, air, and water, which together constitute the totality of manifestation. *The human being is basically an object, according to my concept, a uniquely programmed object.* Let me explain what I mean by programming. The human being had no choice in being born to particular parents, therefore he had no choice about the unique genes or DNA in that human object. For the same reason, he had no choice in being born in a particular environment in which that object has been receiving conditioning from day one. So the unique DNA plus the environmental conditioning is the programming in that object. **Jon Franklin, a Pulitzer Prize Winner, has said it in a picturesque way in his** book, *Molecules of the Mind* **He says, "In the human mechanism there is a mechanism which prevents the human mechanism from seeing its mechanistic nature."** And that mechanism is generally known in the spiritual seeking as the ego.

'Every teaching tells you that the ego is the problem and that you have to kill the ego. So the real question is, where did the ego come from? The ego could not have come from anywhere other than the Source (or God or Consciousness). Where could anything have come from except the Source? For life as we know it to happen, for inter-human relationships to happen, the ego had to be created. It is the ego, the individual thinker, the individual doer, the individual experiencer, who says, "I think, I do, I experience," forgetting the mechanistic nature of the human body-mind organism. The Source had to create the ego so that life could happen as we know it. At the same time, the Source, started the process of destroying the ego in a limited number of cases. Seeking, spiritual seeking, was started at the same time the ego was created.

'This spiritual seeking is an extraordinarily unique seeking. In ordinary seeking in phenomenality, the seeking stops only when the seeker finds the object he is seeking – when he gets what he wants. In the spiritual seeking, the seeking stops the moment the seeker truly understands what it is he is seeking. The rest of the process is purely spontaneous, and has nothing to do with the seeker.

'What does the spiritual seeker really want? He doesn't know. In Bombay when people come to see me, I ask this question regularly. And there is usually no answer, or they say, "That is why I have come to you. There is great confusion about what I am seeking." Or there is an answer, something picked up from some book. "I want to be one with the Oneness." "I want to know the Oneness." "I want to be one with the Source." If the Source is all there is, who is this "one" who wants to be one with Consciousness? The seeking stops the moment it is understood that there never has been a seeker, there never has been a thinker, there never has been a doer of any kind, and there has never been an experiencer. Thinking happens, doing happens, experiencing happens as a matter of the Source functioning through every human being. In other words, no action is an individual's action. It's an action produced by the Source specifically at that time, at that moment, through that specific body-mind organism. And for that to happen, the Source has created the human being with a unique programming so that that particular action at that moment would happen. And the totality of actions through the billions of programmed human objects is the totality of What *Is* at the moment.

'If What Is at the moment is accepted as the will of God, as something which the Source has produced, then there is no happiness or unhappiness. Unhappiness arises because the ego wants something different than What Is at the moment. What the human being is seeking, really, is something which will give him happiness beyond anything that life can give him. That is why the misconception arises that the human being seeks something which transcends life. It is a gross, total misconception. Whatever transcends life is only the Source. The Source is not concerned either with the Truth or with happiness.

'The first thing that the seeker has to find out is whether he or she is seeking anything. Did the seeker start the seeking at a particular time, or did the seeking just happen? In any case it will be found that the seeking was beyond the control of the seeker. When I ask people, "When did you start seeking spiritually?" the usual answer is that they started as far back as they can remember. So my second question to the visitor is, "If the seeking began at an age when most children were seeking something else, why do you suppose this kind of unusual seeking happened to this particular body-mind organism?" The answer is simple. That kind of seeking happened because that kind of program was in that body-mind organism which enabled that type of seeking to happen. In other words, what I am saying is this: Ever since a baby was born and seeks its mother's breast intuitively, life has been nothing but seeking. What kind of seeking depends on the unique programming in that body-mind organism where the seeking happens. Therefore, you find people seeking money, you find people seeking fame, you find people seeking power, and you find people seeking God, or the Source, or the Truth. The choice of the seeking is not with the individual. That kind of seeking happens for which that body-mind organism has been uniquely programmed.

'In the spiritual seeking there are basically three kinds of processes. One is known as bhakti or devotion, and the second is known as jnana or knowledge. There is a third one, called karma, which is selfless action. Even Ramana Maharshi said that bhakti and jnana are two paths leading to the same goal. If someone who has been programmed for bhakti is told about jnana, and circumstances force him to take the path of jnana, there will be conflict. If conflict happens, it could not have happened unless it was the will of God. Likewise, if the seeking takes the particular path for which that particular body-mind organism has been programmed, it is the will of God. In other words, *the third basic concept I have is contained in four simple words: Thy will be done.* That is, nothing can happen unless it is the will of God.

'When something happens, the human being decides whether it is good or bad. When the human being decides that something is good or bad, it is from the point of view of the human being. What is good or bad starts with the individual. "This is good for me, this is good for my family, this is good for my community, this is good for my state, this is good for my country," and this circle expands as the ego becomes more and more magnanimous. The ego says, "What I am trying to do is for the entire human race." But the human race is just a small dot in the totality of the universe. The human being is restricted in his thinking to what is good for himself individually, expanding gradually to the human race. For example: The smallpox germ has been eliminated. Wonderful for the human race – but what about the smallpox germ, which is also part of the existence in the universe? For the smallpox germ it is genocide. So what happens is judged by the human mind only in a very, very restricted way. And, therefore, the human being wants to know why God has done this or God has done that. "Why did God have to produce a Hitler?" The simplest answer is, "Why not?" You can't restrict the power of the Source.

'But the real answer to that is Ramana Maharshi's basic question – Self-inquiry – "Who wants to know?" The one who wants to know is a created object, wanting to know the will of the Creator Subject, which is impossible. When the created object, the human being, wants to know the will of God, what has actually happened is that the created object has usurped the subjectivity of the pure Subject; and what is worse, turned the pure Subjectivity into an object which the pseudo-subject wants to know. Which, according to my concept, is perhaps what could be called the original sin. Therefore, the scientist can succeed only where the "how" of the manifest is concerned, and only that to a limited degree. But he can never know the "why". All that the human being can do is accept the mystery that is the universe. He cannot attempt to solve the mystery. **Meister Eckhart has said it beautifully, "All that one can do is marvel and wonder at the magnificence and diversity of God's creation."** So the acceptance of God's will is the final objective in the spiritual seeking. And that is not in the control of the individual.

'If the individual is so programmed for spiritual seeking that there is enormous receptivity, and the first time this concept [Thy will be done] is put before this body-mind organism, and it goes straight to the heart – of course this can happen. How else can it be? But that kind of receptivity is usually not there. There is a certain resistance. The basic concept, "Thy will be done," is common to every single religion, and yet it is not deeply accepted. Only lip service is done to the Divine, "Thy will be done." But no one, hardly anyone, truly accepts it.

'The seeking stops when the ego realizes what it is that it has been seeking. What is it exactly that the ego has been seeking and the ego has to know? "Thy will be done," meaning the individual free will does not prevail. So the final thing that the ego has to accept is *that it is Consciousness that functions through every human body-mind organism, producing actions at that moment strictly according to the will of God, based on the programming in each human object. That is my basic concept.*

'So, the only sadhana that the ego [seeker] really has to do in this spiritual search, according to my concept, is to find out from personal experience whether any action at any time has been his or her action. The process that I suggest is this: At the end of each day, sit back for ten or twenty or thirty minutes, select a number of actions which have happened that day, simple or complicated actions. Find out whether each one has been your action, or whether it has been an event over which you have had no control. And I daresay that honest investigation, from personal experience, will make it clear to every ego [seeker] that no action that has happened has been his or her action.

'How does an action happen? The Source uses the programmed human computer to bring out an action strictly the way you use your computer. How do you use your computer? You put in an input. The programmed computer has no choice but to bring out an output strictly according to the programming. There is no ego in the computer so the computer doesn't say, "The output is my action." The ego has to find this out from personal experience.

'So what is the input which the Source or God puts in? A thought comes to a human being. He is so used to saying the word "my", that he says, "It is my thought." The thought (or something seen or heard or tasted or smelled or touched) is the Divine input. The human being has no control over what is seen or heard, or what thought is going to come next. That is the input. The brain reacts to that input strictly according to the programming, and the output that comes out is what the human being says is "my" action, or "my" reaction. The same event is seen by three different people with three different programs. The brain will react to that event, and the output could be anger in one case, compassion in the other case, or fear in the third case. The same three reactions could happen even in the case of three sages, because even in the case of a sage, the body-mind organism remains with more or less the same programming.'

CONSCIOUSNESS

Ramesh's first and most basic concept is that Consciousness is all there is:

> The king said to the sage, 'I'll give you half my kingdom if you'll show me where God is.' The sage said to the king, 'I'll give you twice your kingdom if you'll show me where God is not.'

* * *

> In the days of the small kingdoms there was an occasion for celebration. The king and the ministers and all the important people were supposed to get together. So all the people there had been shown their places according to the hierarchy. There was a throne for the king. The chief minister was waiting for the king to arrive, and the ceremony to begin. Suddenly, in walks a Sufi mystic dressed in ragged clothes. He walks straight to the throne and sits down, to the horror of the chief minister. The minister says, 'What do you think you are doing?' The Sufi says, 'I am just sitting here.' So the minister says, 'You aren't even the chief minister because I am the chief minister.' So the Sufi said, 'I am more than the chief minister.' The minister asked, 'Are you the king?' The Sufi replied, 'No, I'm not the king. I'm more than that.' The minister asked, 'Are you the emperor?' The Sufi said, 'I'm not the emperor. I'm more than that.' So the minister said, 'Are you the prophet?' 'No, I'm not the prophet. I'm more than that.' Finally, exasperated, the chief minister said, 'Are you God?' The Sufi replied, 'No, I'm not God. I'm more than that.' The minister, horrified, said, 'But

> more than God means there is nothing!' The Sufi said, 'You are right. I am That nothing.'

The inability to know God's plans led to an interesting discussion between Einstein and Neils Bohr:

> **Neils Bohr and a group of scientists brought the theory of uncertainty, quantum mechanics, to Albert Einstein, then the top physicist in the country. They gave him the theory and begged him to go through it and let them know whether he had any objection to it. Einstein went through it very thoroughly, and found no mistakes. (The theory of uncertainty is that at any moment of time there is a pool of possibilities in the ocean of Consciousness — possibilities, probabilities — out of which, which probability or possibility crystallizes into an action or a thought nobody can know.) Einstein confessed, 'This is absolutely 100 percent tight as a theory. But', he said, 'The theory means that what is going to happen can never be known. Therefore, the implication of the theory is that God plays dice with the universe, and that I cannot accept.' That response was strictly according to Einstein's conditioning. Then Neils Bohr replied to him, 'God is not playing dice with the Universe. You and I may think that God is playing dice with the Universe because we do not have the full information which God has. Our information is from moment to moment. God's information is the eternity.'**

Ramesh has many ways of talking about Consciousness as all there is. 'Consciousness has written the story, Consciousness has made this production, Consciousness is acting all the roles in this drama, and Consciousness is experiencing all the pleasure and the pain through the instruments which are human beings. What is really happening is ever since life began life has always been the existence at the same time of interconnected opposites. Since the story has already been written – all that happens is that the movie is taking place and all we can do is witness it:

> Ramana Maharshi was asked the question, 'The gods and goddesses in the human mythology, are they real?' And his answer was astonishingly accurate. He said, 'Yes, they are as real as you are.'

Ramesh says, 'It is our idea of God, our mental image, that God is all-merciful. So then having created the God, the human being prays to Him. Then, what happens is that he expects God not only to answer the prayers, but he expects the answers to the prayers to be the way he wants:

> There is a story about a man who was wandering about on top of a mountain. He slipped, fell, and grasped the edge of the cliff. He was hanging there. So he shouted to the heavens, 'Is there anyone up there?' There was no answer. So he really prayed. 'Is there anyone, please, up there who can help me?' An answer came. 'Yes, I will help you, but you must do exactly as I say.' The man said, 'Yes. Yes. I will do everything that you say.' The voice said, 'Release your grip.' There was silence. One second. Two seconds. Then the man said, 'Is there anyone else up there?'

Ramesh says, 'God is neither rational nor irrational. God is neither merciful nor unkind. When I use the word God, I do not mean an all-powerful entity, much more powerful than what one is. So how the concept of God came into being is this: The human being felt his or her own helplessness, so the mind-intellect created the concept "God" and went on to give that concept attributes, "all-powerful, all-knowing, all-merciful." So the human intellect gave the attribute "all-merciful" to God, and then asked Him, "Oh, God, why have you created disease and poverty and all these wars?":

A rabbi prided himself in his faith in God. Every now and then he would say, 'I have faith in God.' Once there was a flood. The water was steadily rising. This man sat in his house, and when other people were leaving the area they said to him, 'Come.' But he said, 'No. I will stay here. I have faith in God.' The waters kept rising. Then a boat came. The people in the boat said, 'Look, we have room for one more. Better come with us. The water is rising.' The man said, 'No. I have faith in God.' So the boat went. Another boat came. He said the same thing, 'Nope, I won't go with you. I have faith in God.' Finally a helicopter came. They said, 'Look, this is your last chance. We'll throw you a rope. Climb up and get in, otherwise there will be no more help coming.' The man said, 'No, I have faith in God.' The waters kept rising, and, of course, the man drowned. So when he met God in heaven he asked God, 'I had faith in you. Why did you let me drown?' God told him, 'I tried to help you three times. I sent you a boat twice. I even sent you a helicopter!'

The nature of reality becomes part of the discussion about Consciousness. The questioners inquire from the point of view that what they experience through their senses is what is real. Ramesh responds by talking about how the human being is a body-mind organism being operated by Consciousness; often comparing the body-mind apparatus to an electrical appliance and Consciousness to the electricity that operates it:

> When I was twelve years old in school we had a physiology teacher. He drew a diagram on the blackboard illustrating that the lens of a camera and the lens of our eye are identical in the sense that the object is formed on the lens and on the cornea. That seemed clear enough. But at that moment my mind

wandered, and the teacher came to me. He thought I was dreaming, so he said, 'What did I say?' I repeated exactly what he had said. He was a bit surprised, so he said, 'What were you thinking about?' I said I had a question. He said, 'What is the question?' I said, 'In the camera someone has to click the button before the object in the lens gets registered on the film. So in the eye which sees an object and the object is reflected in the cornea, who does the clicking?' He was very angry and he said, 'Don't ask stupid questions.' I said, 'Fine.' But later on when Maharaj was talking about Consciousness being everything and that all actions are merely appearances in Consciousness, I was suddenly reminded of that memory and I said, 'Now I know who does the clicking.'

* * *

One day Chuang Tzu came to his disciples. He said, 'I am worried. I am concerned.' So his disciples said, 'What is happening?' Chuang Tzu said, 'I dreamt last night that I was, a butterfly.' His disciples said, 'Master, it's only a dream.' So he said, 'I know it's only a dream, and I knew that when I woke up. But my problem is, am I Chuang Tzu who dreamt last night that I was a butterfly; or is the butterfly now dreaming that he is Chuang Tzu?'

Maya is a Sanskrit word for illusion, the veiling power that conceals the real and projects the unreal. The Hindu religion views what happens here on earth as the maya, the grand illusion, the grand play:

> I had a science teacher once when I was in school. He said, 'Maya, maya, what nonsense! You go and hit your head against the wall. Do you not get hurt? Where is the maya?' At that moment I thought — but I have

always been a timid person and I didn't have the guts to ask him — 'Doesn't the same thing happen in your dream? You hit your head on the wall and your head gets hurt. But it's still in the dream.'

❈ ❈ ❈

Some years ago I came across a very good short novel called *Colossus*. Later, someone told me that a movie had been made of it. The whole point of the novel was that the United States developed a super computer, which will take into account everything. The president doesn't have to decide on anything. So, ultimately, after very deep consultations, the president presses the button and the computer begins to work. The first thing the computer says is, 'There is another.' It keeps on saying, 'There is another.' Apparently Russia has also developed an identical computer. The two computers interact and decide that there has to be one. So the United states and Russia build the Colossus, which is in charge of the world. If Colossus decides something and if any human being or any nation opposes it, it gives a warning. Its threat is carried out. So, ultimately the American scientist who developed the American super computer becomes so exasperated that he asks the Colossus, 'Who are you?' The Colossus says, 'I am God. And you will soon get used to the idea.'

A more compassionate view is presented in the following story, called *Footprints* by Margaret Powers, which Ramesh tells at almost every seminar. Several times I have witnessed him choke up and become overwhelmed with tears as he tells it:

> A good, God-fearing man dreamt that he was walking across the sands of a desert with God. That walk was synonymous with the life story of the man. As both

walked along, the two pairs of feet made two trails of footprints in the sand. But at times the man could see only one pair of footsteps. He then asked God, 'Dear God, why is it that at times there is only one trail in the sand? I see that the other trail is missing at the times when I went through great despair and agony in my life. Why, when I needed you the most, you were not with me?' God looked with great compassion at the man and He replied, 'My dear friend, it is true that there is only one trail of footprints in the sand during the most difficult times of your life. But during those times, it was I who carried you in my arms.'

Ramesh says that Consciousness is both innate in phenomenality, and at the same time, transcendent. He illustrates that concept with the following saying from the Tao in Chinese philosophy:

First the rivers and mountains are real, then the rivers and mountains are unreal, and then the rivers and mountains are real.

At first there is total involvement – 'I' am different from the rivers and mountains. Then comes the stage where it is seen to be an illusion, when the rivers and mountains are no longer rivers and mountains. Then finally, when this 'me' becomes part of the rivers and mountains which are no longer seen as rivers and mountains, then the rivers and mountains are again seen as rivers and mountains. The circle is complete. The rivers and mountains are then perceived as real phenomenal objects in which the Consciousness is innate. They're real, and at the same time they are unreal because they can't exist by themselves.

NO PERSONAL DOER, NO INDIVIDUAL 'ME'

Ramesh says again and again, 'That is the only knowledge you truly have, "I Am." That "I-I", which is the unmanifest manifesting Itself as the appearance in Consciousness, "I Am," is the universal Consciousness that is present in every body-mind organism. The separation comes when the "I Am" becomes "I am John" and that separation is the cause of all the bondage and misery':

> A Sufi was stoned to death and went to heaven. Not long after, a man who had witnessed that death also died and went to heaven. He was indignant to find that the Sufi was also there. He inquired of God, 'Why is this Sufi here in heaven, and the Pharaoh, who said the same thing, is in hell?' God replied, 'When the Pharaoh said he was God, he was thinking of himself. When the Sufi said he was God, he was thinking of Me.'

❊ ❊ ❊

Ramana Maharshi says that all that needs to be done is to find out who wants enlightenment. 'Who am I? Who is doing the seeking? Who wants to know?' If you delve deep into this series of questions, you will come to the conclusion that there is no 'who'. Not many people can accept it. Ramana Maharshi compared the seekers who can come to this acceptance to camphor, dry wood, or wet wood. The camphor needs just a spark to ignite. The dry wood needs a certain amount of warming. The wet wood needs a tremendous amount of warming before it catches fire.

The following incident illustrates how easy it is to get confused about who or what the 'me' is and is not:

> There was one gentleman who attended the talks who was very learned. He was a school teacher who had retired early just to think about the nature of reality. He thought about it and came to the conclusion that all this is just a dream of his. So he started saying, 'If I am a dreamer...' Normally, I don't interrupt, but somehow at that moment I said, 'Harry, you are not the dreamer...' Harry looked intense. For a moment I thought he had taken offense. Then other questions came up from others. Later he came to me and said, 'Ramesh, that's all I needed.' I said, 'You are not the dreamer, you are a dreamed character as Harry. You are the dreamer, but not as Harry.' There were hardly any more questions from him.

Questions about rebirth, karma, and other concepts that represent the persistence and the continuation of the individual 'me', arise throughout the seminar. This arising is stimulated by the mind of, the individual, unable to see itself not existing:

> The Buddha has clearly put it, 'As there is no self, there is no transmigration of self, but there are beings and continued effects of beings. There are deeds being done, but there is no doer. There is no entity that migrates. No self is transferred from one place to another, but there is a voice uttered here and the echo of it comes back.'

Ramesh also quotes Ramana Maharshi as saying, **'There was no rebirth, there is no rebirth, there will never be rebirth — this is the truth!'**

FREE WILL

'"I am an individual with freedom of choice and action." This is what the me says. This feeling of independent choice and action is what constitutes an individual.' Ramesh illustrates this point by saying, 'No person has the choice of being born. We have no choice over our genes, and no choice regarding the conditioning which each one of us has received in the environment in which we were born. We are not going to have any choice about death. In between these two determinate events over which we have had no choice – birth and death – what right do I have to think that I have the free will to do as I want? Where does the question of choice come in? So, other than surrendering to God, what alternative do we have?'

One of the basic points that Ramesh pursues under the notion of free will is that whatever is supposed to happen will happen, and that is not in our hands:

> **I'll tell you what happened to my brother once. He had an appointment to keep so he was walking briskly. One of his friends called him, so he had to stop. When the friend came over to him, my brother had to explain that he was in a terrible hurry and he would call him later. It must have taken a few seconds. Then he went ahead. A little while later he saw an enormous stone fall from a construction site right where he would have been walking a few seconds earlier. So it could be that if his friend had not stopped him he could have been under that stone.**

❋ ❋ ❋

There was an Arabian sage named Manoimus who said, 'Ask yourself whence is it that you would rather sleep when you are awake, and why is it that you are awake

when you want to sleep. Ask yourself whence is it that you fall in love when you would rather not — and when you inquire into all these things you will come to the correct answer that you have no free will.

'When someone asked about free will and predetermination, Ramana Maharshi said, "Everything that happens is predetermined." And then someone among the visitors raised his arm and said, "Bhagavan, I raised my hand. Surely that is my action and it could not have been predetermined. Or is that also predetermined?" And Ramana Maharshi merely said, "Yes". That man didn't pursue it further and frankly I don't know what Ramana Maharshi would have said or done if this man had asked, "How could that have been? I raised my arm." In this case the matter was not pursued, but if it were pursued here, my answer would be very simple. "You think you raised your arm." Ramana Maharshi said, "Every action, every deed that happens is predetermined." So that is something that was heard. The brain reacted to what was heard and the reaction was, "How can you say it is not my action?" And the arm was raised – a purely mechanical reaction of the brain to what was heard, "Everything is predetermined."'

Ramesh says, 'The brain is not a creative matter; it is only a receptive apparatus. The brain can only react to a thought or an outside event. **The brain surgeon Benjamin Libet reportedly said, "A thought which you consider as your thought occurs fully a half second before you consider it your thought."** So what you call your action is really a reaction of the brain to a thought or to something that you see or hear. The brain cannot create a thought; the brain can only receive a thought. The thought that comes can only come from the Self, from Consciousness, from God':

> I read an account the other day of the British physicist-astronomer Fred Hoyle. He said he was attending a conference of physicists in Paris. There was a problem he wanted to deal with at the conference, and he

didn't have a solution. He had been thinking it over for many days and nights. And then, as he says, the solution occurred to him suddenly when he was crossing the street in Paris. It arose in his mind. He had no question in his mind about the solution; in fact, he didn't even bother to rush to his hotel room and write it down because he knew that it couldn't change. So he went through the day, and at the end of it when he reached his hotel room, he wrote down the solution in mathematical terms, which took him quite some time. That solution, which took him some time to put down on paper, came to him suddenly.

Ramesh says that any particular body-mind organism is given certain characteristics and traits, which make it possible for what is going to occur through that body-mind organism to occur:

> Who can do anything? Only the Source can do anything. What that doing is may be anything. What that doing is could be murder. When the Israeli prime minister was killed the other day, the young man who shot him was asked, 'Why did you shoot him?' His answer to the best of my recollection was, 'God made me do it.' And he is strictly, accurately correct.

Ramesh tells the following joke about the programming of a body-mind organism:

> A man went into a bar. The barman offered him a drink. He said, 'I tried it once, I didn't like it.' The barman offered him a smoke. He said, 'I tried it once, I didn't like it.' Then the man said, 'But wait a minute. My son will be here in a minute and he will share a drink and a smoke with you.' The barman replied, 'Your only son, no doubt?'

Whether a body-mind organism is going to die a natural death, or by accident or murder or suicide — it's the same thing. Someone who has been coming to me for many years was a policeman. But he was programmed not to be a policeman. He was too sensitive. The result was that there was a nervous breakdown. So, fortunately for him the government recognized whatever proof he gave, and now he gets a pension. But the story he told me is that at one point during his nervous breakdown he was sitting in his living room and he decided to shoot himself. The situation was so bad and he couldn't bear his life. On his way to the cupboard where he kept his gun he said he heard a voice distinctly saying, 'Don't do this.' The voice was so compelling that he stood in his tracks and he did not commit suicide. The destiny of that body-mind organism was not to commit suicide.

❋ ❋ ❋

Seals in the Arctic were being clubbed and killed. The scene was witnessed on television by J. Krishnamurti. Krishnamurti has gone on record to say that the scene was so horrible for him — he had a very sensitive body and mind — that he went and switched off the television program. The same scene was witnessed by the famous actress Bridget Bardot, and she couldn't sleep nights. Bridget Bardot organized a movement which became so strong that ultimately this practice of hitting baby seals on the head was stopped by the government. It was part of the role of Krishnamurti not to play an active role in this, whereas Bridget Bardot had an active role.

When he is speaking on the subject of free will, Ramesh frequently quotes Dr. Stanley Milgrim's experiments because they show how easily influenced a human being can be:

> Dr. Milgrim conducted some highly original experiments at the psychology department of Yale University some years ago. The purpose was to discover the limits of the average person's obedience to authority when ordered to inflict severe pain on an innocent victim by electric shocks. The consensus of 39 psychiatrists who were consulted before the experiment was that most subjects would not go beyond 150 volts when the victim, a professional actor, asked for the first time to be released. They expected that only 4 percent would reach 300 volts, and that only a pathological fringe of about one in a thousand, would administer the highest shock of about 450 volts on the board. In actual fact, over 60 percent of the subjects at Yale continued to obey to the very end of the 450 volt limit — the maximum pain that could be inflicted. And it must be made clear that the supervising authority had no power over his volunteer subjects, comparable to an army officer or even a schoolteacher. They were volunteers and all they were told was that this experiment was in the interest of a noble cause.
>
> In another series of experiments in which the subject was told that he was free to inflict on the victim any shock level of his own choice, the astonishing revelation was that almost all subjects administered the lowest shocks on the control panel. The mean shock level being 54 volts. The victim's mild complaint began only at 75 volts. So left to themselves, the volunteer subjects would inflict only 54 volts when the sense of responsibility was there. But under instructions from an authority, they went as high as

450 volts. It was conclusively proved that it was not any innate aggressiveness that transforms harmless citizens into torturers, but their self-transcending devotion to a cause, symbolized by the leader. It is the integrative tendency acting as a vehicle or a catalyst which induces the change of morality, the abrogation of personal responsibility, the replacement of the individual's code of behavior by the code of the higher component in the hierarchy.

The final conclusion which Dr. Milgrim drew from his experiment was, 'This is perhaps the most fundamental lesson of our study. Ordinary people, simply doing their jobs and without any particular hostility on their parts, can become agents in a terrible destructive process. Moreover, even when the destructive effects of their work become potently clear and they were asked to carry out actions incompatible with fundamental standards of morality, relatively few people had the internal resources needed to resist authority. It is ironic that the virtues of loyalty, discipline and self-sacrifice that we value so highly in the individual, are the very properties that create destructive organizational engines of war and bind them to malevolent systems of authority.'

At the seminars Ramesh often says that everyone who is supposed to be there is there, and everyone who is not supposed to be there is not there:

> When I mentioned this in Aspen, Colorado, someone couldn't help laughing. So everyone looked at him. He was embarrassed. He said, 'I'm sorry. I didn't mean to disturb, but let me explain what has happened.' He said that just the previous day he was flying from New York to Denver. It was a long flight and he didn't have

enough to read. He noticed that his neighbor was reading all the while from a book. When the neighbor left his seat, he picked up the book and started reading. He was so involved in the reading that he didn't realize that his neighbor had returned. He was very embarrassed and he apologized. The neighbor said, 'Well, I've read it several times. You read it as long as you want to.' So he read it for about half an hour or an hour and said to his neighbor, 'I would like to meet the author.' The neighbor said, 'Would you really? That's where I'm going.' So he said he got off at Denver, got an appropriate ticket to Aspen, and he said, 'Here I am,' and pointing to the man next to him, 'And this is my neighbor on the plane.'

✻ ✻ ✻

Someone asked me once — she spoke very softly, she didn't mean to be impertinent — 'Why are you here?' She said it so softly I didn't hear it, so I said, 'I beg your pardon?' She said, 'Why are you here?' Really, what she wanted to know was why she was here. I said, 'I am here for the simple reason that you are here. Neither you nor I at this moment could have been anywhere else in the world. We had to be here. As part of the here and now we had to be here.' And then she explained that she didn't mean to be there. She was supposed to be somewhere else, and somehow, something happened that she was there. And a friend of hers who was supposed to come with her didn't come. So the friend of hers who was supposed to be there was not there; and she was not supposed to be there and she was there! What she was hearing was making an impact on her; she was terribly confused. So her mind said, 'Why am I here? What is being said? How am I concerned?' Nevertheless, the impact was happening.

When talking about free will and predetermination, Ramesh says that everything has already happened. He likens this notion to a huge painting ten miles long and over five hundred feet high, and says you can't see the whole picture, only the part that is in front of you:

> In the Bhagavad Gita, Arjuna as a seeker, said, 'I see before me my cousins and my preceptors as my enemy. How can I kill them?' Lord Krishna tells Arjuna, 'You may decide not to fight, but that decision will be futile. The programming that made this body-mind organism a born warrior, trained to be a warrior, will not allow you not to fight. You may decide not to fight but it will be futile. I have already killed them. Therefore, win the war, and enjoy the fruits of victory.'

✸ ✸ ✸

Stephen Hawking, the mathematician, has written an essay called, 'Is Everything Predetermined?' That essay is about twelve pages long and very interesting. Ultimately, what interested me most was the final paragraph of three lines. He began the paragraph with the line, 'Is everything predetermined? The answer is yes.' Then he said, 'But it won't help you because you'll never know what it is.'

✸ ✸ ✸

There was a Zen master who had a young grandson who would listen to him. So once the grandson broke a crystal vase that the grandfather greatly valued. Before the grandfather could discover it, the grandson went to his grandfather and said, 'Remember, Grandfather, you said everybody has a certain span of life?' The grandfather said, 'Yes.' 'Well,' said the grandson, 'the span of life of that crystal vase is over.'

There is a very interesting story about Nostradamus, the great seer. A count in his territory had heard about Nostradamus and his fame as a seer, so he called him for dinner one day along with several of his friends. He wanted to expose Nostradamus as a fraud, so he told his cook, 'Stay back and listen to what he says, and then do the opposite.' The count then told Nostradamus, 'The cook has a white pig and a black pig. Which pig is going to come on the table?' Nostradamus said, 'The white pig.' The cook overheard this and began to cook the black pig. When the pig came on the table the count asked the cook, 'Which pig is that?' The cook replied, 'The white pig.' The count was flabbergasted. He said, 'You were supposed to cook the black pig.' The cook said, 'Yes, I did cook the black pig. But two wolves came from outside and took the pig away, so I had to cook the white pig. That's why I was a bit late.'

Ramesh said at one seminar, 'There is good news and bad news. This is the bad news – that "You" can do nothing. But don't forget the good news. When you can truly accept that there is nothing "you" can do, that it may be that things are just happening and "I" am not in control of my life, then this kind of understanding brings about no guilt, no pride, no hate or envy. That is the good news.'

Ramesh finds that people's reactions vary greatly to the notion that they have no free will:

> I was talking about no free will. I had a Dutch woman on my right and an American woman on my left. As soon as we stopped talking the Dutch woman said, 'This gives me a tremendous sense of freedom.' And almost in the same breath, spontaneously, the American woman said, 'This gives me a tremendous feeling of helplessness!'

As the discussion of free will continues, several very predictable questions arise from the seekers, or Ramesh brings them up. 'If you accept that all actions which happen through any body-mind organism are not truly anyone's actions, but are God's actions, the mind promptly raises several objections. One objection is, "If nothing is in my hands why should I do anything? Why should I not remain idle?"' To which Ramesh replies, 'The point is that you cannot remain idle. There is energy within each body-mind organism, and that energy will not allow that body-mind organism to remain idle. The second objection is, "If nothing is in my hands, I could easily go and commit a murder." The answer is that it is not as easy as that to go and commit a murder. If the natural characteristic of your organism is such that you are not a violent person, then such a murder will not take place. Another objection is, you say if "God has done it, why should I be punished?" But the point is if any action that is produced by God through a body-mind organism is not his action but an action over which he has no control, then all consequences are strictly happening according to the destiny of that organism':

> **Ramakrishna Paramahansa's teaching was basically bhakti, but deep down his was also Advaitic teaching. Someone asked him, 'I am a simple man. I would like to be told what to do. Can you give me a simple formula for how to live my life?' The answer was amazingly simple. Ramakrishna said, 'Totally accept that you are only a machine operated upon by God, and then you may do whatever you like.'**

'The ultimate question is, "What do I do from now on?" The ultimate answer to that ultimate question is extraordinarily simple: You keep on doing what you think you have been doing so far':

> **There is a wonderful line from the American poet, e.e. cummings: 'If you can just be, be. If not, cheer up and**

go about other people's business, doing and undoing unto them until you drop.'

Ramesh says that one must act as if one has free will. But ultimately, the free will is counterfeit. He explains that it is your free will to make a decision at any moment, but whether the outcome of that decision works out as you want it to is not in your control:

Suppose you found a lot of money in the attic and you were delighted. But when you went to spend the money you found out that it was counterfeit and you couldn't use it. Free will is like that; it is counterfeit.

THE 'ME' OR THE EGO

Ramesh defines a healthy ego as 'one that realizes it is not perfect, and that the world is made up of interconnected opposites, and accepts this'. He says that the 'me' and the belief in free will are synonymous. 'As the understanding that there is no free will goes deeper, the "me" becomes weaker.'

'Consciousness has brought about the identification with each body-mind organism through the mechanism of the mind. The mind, or the ego, is truly the cause of the separation; and it is not due to any fault of the human being. The ego has to be accepted as part of the functioning of Totality. What this separation has brought about is a sense of independence. The same Consciousness which has created the separation, has also created the illusion of being in charge – not only being in charge of the world, but being in charge of ourselves.'

The following stories illustrate how the mind judges and separates as part of its nature. 'The stronger the ego is – the stronger its belief in itself as causal and all-knowing – the bigger the difficulty in accepting its limitations':

> A certain king wanted to live forever. He searched his kingdom for someone who could make him immortal. Finally a sage came forward and said that he had a potion for immortality, and whoever drank it would never die. There was only one condition. The king must drink it twice a day, and he was never to think of a monkey while he drank it.

✸ ✸ ✸

> A Buddhist master read aloud a text. It was a very beautiful text and everybody was much impressed. But

promptly the question came, 'Who wrote it?' So the master said, 'If I told you that the Buddha wrote it you would venerate it, you would worship it, you would put flowers on it every morning and bow down to it. If I told you that a patriarch had written it, you would still give it great respect, but you would not venerate it as you would if the Buddha had written it. If I told you that a monk had written it, you wouldn't know how to react. And if I told you that our cook had written it, you would laugh.'

❋ ❋ ❋

In Maharaj's talks a person used to come who had the unusual record of being first in every exam from the first exam in primary school to his master's degree — not just first in class, but the top in every examination. Maharaj knew about this achievement. So Maharaj almost literally threw up his hands when this person asked him, 'I take your word for it that that is the supreme state, but how do I know that I am going to enjoy that state?' Maharaj asked me afterwards, 'How can it be? I can't understand it. A man with such intellect, with such academic achievement, that he should ask that question, forgetting the whole point — that in that state there can be no "me" to ask the question.'

Ramesh says that 'the ego depends on its programming and conditioning to react. The involvement happens according to the destiny and the programming.' He used the following story to illustrate this point:

> Two men are going along together. A woman happens to be molested nearby. The programming in one body-mind organism is to be timid. He will hesitate. The other one is programmed to be courageous. He will go

and try to rescue the woman, and in trying to rescue her will hit the man and injure him. Then he is taken before a judge and jury. In the case of an ordinary man, he will think, 'Why did I interfere?' What has actually happened is that he had no choice in his action. In the case of a sage, he will sit there quietly knowing that it is the destiny of that body-mind organism to be where it is at the present moment. He will accept it.

The self-centeredness of the human ego also elicits stories. 'Basically, whatever the human being wants at the highest level is still selfish. When a man says he wants what he wants for himself and the whole world, he thinks he has reached a tremendous height of being unselfish. But the human being thinking from the point of view of the human being is still selfish because he doesn't think in terms of the millions of other species':

> I was reading some time ago some instances about Swami Nityananda Maharaj in Ganeshpuri, about 50 miles from Bombay. He is the guru of Swami Muktananda, who is more well known. Swami Nityananda used to have a fairly large crowd and everyone would bring some flowers or fruits. Every evening Nityananda would tell his attendant to send this to that temple, or that to this group. Once it so happened that some fruit remained overnight and in the heat of India, the fruit went bad. So the attendant complained to him the next morning, 'See, you didn't tell me where to send this and it remained overnight and now it has gone bad.' I was greatly struck by Nityananda's reply. He said, 'Don't worry, the fruits have gone exactly where they are supposed to go.' (To the worms!)

The 'Me' or the Ego

Another point that Ramesh makes about the ego is that it is afraid of change, and yet the nature of reality is that everything changes. The following anecdotes illustrate this point:

> Where I live it was originally one big flat, and we turned it into two for my brother and me. There used to be a veranda open to the sky, and it was wonderful. Apart from the three months of monsoon, we practically lived there in the mornings and the evenings, particularly in the evenings. But it had to be covered with a cement sheet, which created a roof. When there was a storm, the air used to get in between and create a tremendous sound, a fearful sound. There was always a sense that one of these days that damn thing was going to fly off. Every time the thought came it would get cut off, but nonetheless it would come. One time there was a storm and that part of the roof did blow off! I stood there and watched it. My wife went to the phone. I said, 'Why are you getting in a panic? The world doesn't have to know about one piece of the Balsekar roof that has flown off.' So, what seemed like a calamity, when it really happened, was all right. The rain did come through and we had to move the furniture, but it wasn't the end of the world.

❋ ❋ ❋

Most of the fears that happen are based on memory; they are purely a creation of the mind. As someone said in the seminar in South India, 'I've had a terrible life. Most of it didn't happen!'

THE THINKING MIND
AND THE WORKING MIND

Ramesh developed the concepts of the thinking mind and the working mind to help clarify people's confusions about different states of being. He said, 'The working mind is only concerned with the job being done. The thinking mind is concerned with the consequences in the future. That is the big difference. It is the nature of the thinking mind to come and interrupt the working mind. The thinking mind is the ego. The working mind is not the ego. So when Enlightenment or Self-realization or Total Understanding happens, the working mind has to continue, otherwise the body-mind organism of the sage would not be able to function':

> There is a saying among the adepts, 'Trust in Allah, but tether your camel.' In modern terms that would be, 'Trust in God, but don't forget to lock up your car and take the keys.'

❋ ❋ ❋

> I read the other day a story about Winston Churchill. He owned a racehorse that was expected to win the Derby. He didn't win; he came in fourth. Churchill had his own excuse. He said, 'I know why he didn't win. just before the race I told him, 'This is the one final race. You win this race and you'll not have to race anymore. You will have the best of female company for the rest of your life.' He said, 'That was a mistake. The horse did not have his mind on the job.'

❋ ❋ ❋

> My concept is that most of the successful men in any area are those who are not necessarily the most brilliant in their professional occupation, but where it so happens by God's grace and the destiny of that body-mind organism that the thinking mind doesn't interrupt the working mind. That's why I'm told the famous ballet dancer Nijinski is reported to have said, 'Nijinski dances best when Nijinski is not there.'

This seems to be Ramesh's favorite illustration of the working mind-thinking mind concept, judging by how often he tells it, and how much enjoyment the audience gets from hearing it:

> Two men are named Mutt and Jeff. They are from an American cartoon strip. I don't know if it exists anymore, because I haven't seen it for a long time. I think Mutt is the short one and Jeff is the tall one. Jeff is driving them in a car up a hill, and they are going very, very slowly. Jeff is leaning forward in the car as if to help it up the hill. They finally get slowly to the top and Jeff says, 'Whew, Mutt. That was scary. We could have slipped and slid backward down the hill.' Mutt replied, 'No worry. I had the handbrake on all the time.'

WITNESSING

'Witnessing means that there is no involvement. Witnessing can happen with even the smallest intellectual understanding.' Ramesh illustrates the different states of 'being' through this anecdote:

> Henry Dennison used to come see me in Bombay around eleven o'clock. The door of the apartment was open. He would come in the elevator, walk through the door, and I would be waiting for him. One day he came in and he saw me sitting in the rocking chair with my eyes closed, so he tiptoed to his seat and sat down. I don't know how long, maybe a few minutes later, I opened my eyes and saw Henry sitting. Henry promptly said, 'Before we say anything else, tell me what state you were in when I came in.' I said, 'I hadn't thought about it, but now that you ask I think what was happening was what usually happens. When there is something to be witnessed, witnessing is taking place constantly. But when there is nothing to witness, then the witnessing state deepens into a non-witnessing state. In the non-witnessing state the sounds are heard, the traffic on the road is heard, the smells are smelled, but in a very, very passive way. They do not produce any reaction. If there is something which needs witnessing, the transition from the non-witnessing to the witnessing state is extremely smooth, like the automatic changing of the gears in a car. It's spontaneous and very, very smooth. If the non-witnessing state continues without disturbance for awhile, then that non-witnessing state goes deeper so even those sounds and smells which earlier were passively noted, are no longer noted. This is what has been happening.' And curiously, that same

evening, I picked up a book on Ramana Maharshi, an excellent book by a man called David Godman. I opened the book (and by now I've given up using the word 'coincidence') and the question that struck my eye was this one that was being asked of Ramana Maharshi. 'I sometimes get into a state of mind where I'm conscious of the sounds and smells, but in an extremely passive way. Please tell me if this is the mind deceiving itself, or is it a good state to be in?' Ramana Maharshi said, 'That is precisely the state to be aimed at.' He called that state the 'natural state'.

❈ ❈ ❈

In my flat for some reason or other, the door's never been locked so friends and neighbors just push the door and come in. As soon as they enter there is a very large mirror. I can sit in the rocking chair and see people coming and going. It's quite interesting. Someone pushes the door and comes in. He sees the reflection in the mirror but it's only witnessed. There's no reaction. Then he takes a step or two, and suddenly realizes that it's been his image and then he is startled. In the beginning it is just witnessing, but the moment the mind focuses the attention, the witnessing is gone and the mind becomes involved.

Ramesh uses the illustration of a baby to explain witnessing. He says, 'When a baby is content – she has had her milk, her diapers are changed – just watch the baby's expression. It is most interesting. It is not that the look is unintelligent. The look takes in what is there, what is witnessed, and the baby reacts to what is witnessed. You make faces at her and she will cry. You smile at her; she'll smile. The smile and the crying are the reactions of the body-mind organism to the outside event, which is merely witnessed. She doesn't say, "That bearded man frightens me; that other man is a nice man, he doesn't frighten me. He makes me smile." That is a judgment which a baby does not make.' Ramesh often tells this story about witnessing pain:

> I had an operation for the removal of my appendix many years ago. At that time I didn't have my earlier guru; this was back in 1948. The surgeon warned me, 'There will be pain, but the nurse has been instructed to give you a further injection so you will be all right.' I had this sense of satisfaction that the nurse was there; but somehow at that point the thought came, 'Let me see what this pain is.' So when the pain started, I thought, 'The pain has started.' There was no panic. It may be because I knew that I had the injection ready any time that I wanted. Indeed, it was that fact that made me go through with this experiment. Gradually that pain increased, and that pain was being watched until the pain leveled off. The thought came to me, 'If this pain, which has leveled off, had been there with me all the time, ever since I was born, I would have accepted it as part of this organism.' I was operated upon at eight o'clock in the morning. This witnessing went on right up to six o'clock in the evening. Then the nurse came and said that she would give me the injection and my food so that I would sleep well. I said, 'Fine. My experiment is over.' She mentioned this to the surgeon. He said, 'I didn't realize you had such a capacity to bear pain.' I said, 'Doctor, my own feeling has always been that my capacity to bear pain is much less than the average person.'

This next anecdote illustrates how the thinking mind interferes with the state of witnessing, or as Ramesh puts it, the reaction to the reaction:

> A friend of mine lost his wife after fifty-five years of marriage. When I went to see him after ten or twelve

days, he was again overcome with feelings. And he had the idea that he had the Understanding, that he knew what It was all about. He had been reading books for forty years. So he told me, 'All that reading, all that knowledge of forty years was found useless when the chips were down.' When his wife died he was overcome with grief, and every time someone came to sympathize with him the emotions overwhelmed him again. He said, 'Now, when you have come, it is still there, after nearly two weeks. And I thought I was a jnani. I thought I had understood.' At that time to speak to him on this matter would have been to add insult to injury. So I didn't speak to him then. But when I went home somehow I went straight to my desk and wrote him a longish letter. I concluded by saying, 'I presume you have read this. Please forgive the impertinence, and just throw it away.' But I wrote because it was almost compulsive. What I wrote to him was this: 'Your reaction to the death of your wife was a perfectly normal reaction for the body-mind organism in question. You love your wife; you miss your wife. That's all there is. So the reaction to the death of your wife is perfectly natural, perfectly spontaneous. What is perhaps wrong is your reaction to that reaction. You are reacting to that reaction saying, "I thought I was a jnani and here I am groveling in grief." So that reaction is what is incorrect.' And that reaction really proves that his understanding was not deep enough. So I wrote and said, 'If you had not loved your wife as much as you did, then probably her death would not have affected you as much. And then you probably would have thought, "I know what it's all about. I am a jnani. The death of my wife doesn't mean so much. I accept it." But that reaction would not have been because of being a jnani, it would have been because you didn't love your wife!'

CHILDREN AND THEIR UNDERSTANDING

The insight that children have is really amazing. Ramesh frequently tells this story about his granddaughter:

> Akshata was a restless child. One evening her mother was absolutely tired so she told Akshata — a very intelligent child — 'Look, Akshata, at the end of the day you have made me so tired. You must do something so you don't make me so tired.' Akshata agreed. 'Yes mother. Anything you wish.' So her mother said, 'I'll give you a bath and after the bath you go to your room, sit for five minutes and pray to God that he makes you a good girl.' She said, 'I'll do it!' So she went to her room. She came back after five minutes and she said, 'Mommy. I prayed really hard. I don't want to make you tired, so I prayed really hard.' The next day, the same thing happened. So her mother said, 'Akshata, I thought you had prayed to God.' Akshata said, 'Mommy, I did pray hard. And if He hasn't made me a good girl either He can do nothing about it, or He wants me to be what I am.'

✻ ✻ ✻

In Los Angeles we had a lovely cook. It was an open space and you could hear the gentle sound of things being mixed and she could listen to the talks. I would often see her coming out of the gap and standing there and listening. At a certain point I used to narrate the story of my granddaughter and the child's intuitive insight into the truth. At that time I must have mentioned the story three or four times on previous days, and I was just about to skip it and she knew it. She said, 'Tell them about your granddaughter! Tell them about your granddaughter!'

✸ ✸ ✸

Eva Marie had four children. A woman, Karen, was employed to look after the children and after the house. Karen left when Eva Marie came back at five o'clock in the evening. So one day Karen said to Eva Marie, 'Do you know what Philip told me today? He said, "We are all dreaming and we'll wake up when we are dead."' Philip was five or six years old. Eva Marie thought, 'There must be something wrong.' So after she had given him a bath and was drying him, she asked, 'What did you talk to Karen about?' Philip said, 'We talked about lots of things.' Eva Marie asked, 'About dreaming and waking?' 'Oh yes. I told Karen we are all dreaming and we'll wake up when we are dead.' Absolutely accurate. So she asked, 'Who told you that?' And Eva Marie told me, 'The way he looked at me with such compassion, that I should ask such a stupid question, "Who told you that?" But I didn't take back my question, so Philip said, "Who told me that? God told me that."'

When Ramesh told that story in Hollywood, someone else volunteered another that he now includes in his talks:

> This story appeared in a parenting or family magazine. A woman had a new baby girl and the baby had an older brother, about two or three years old, who could walk and talk. The mother found him in his sister's crib, asking the baby, 'Tell me about God. I seem to be forgetting.'

CONCEPTS

'Everything is a concept. Never forget that. Everything is a concept, so don't be afraid of using concepts. Concepts are necessary. **Ramana Maharshi made it beautifully clear. He said, "You use a concept like a thorn to remove another thorn imbedded in your foot. When you remove it, you throw both thorns away."** Then you are free of concepts. But if you carry one concept, then you carry a load of concepts which hide the truth. So, by all means, use a concept. But once you have used a concept, throw it away.'

'The process of the human mind precludes the seeing of interrelated opposites. Usually the mind goes towards one or the other. Therefore the complementary nature of most things is not seen. A concept can be interpreted either way':

> **Two monks in training were passionate smokers and they found great difficulty in sitting in meditation. When they discussed it between themselves and could not come to a conclusion, they decided to ask their own respective superiors. The next day they met to find out what had happened. The first monk said, 'Well, I asked my superior and he was very angry that I should even ask the question.' The other monk said, 'That's surprising. I asked my superior, "Can I pray when I'm smoking?" and he said, "Certainly, my son."'** Then he said to the other monk, 'What did you ask?' He replied, 'I asked whether I can smoke when I'm praying.'

INTERRELATED OPPOSITES

'Another question that arises when the mind tries to accept that it has no free will is, "Why have I chosen to be independent and separate?" The answer is that it is not your choice. It is part of the functioning of Totality. If we accept what is, there is no problem, no difficulty. Whenever we want something different, the problems arise. But I am going a step further – the problems are supposed to arise. Life is interconnected opposites. It is totally futile to expect that there would be only good in this life':

> A Sufi saying: 'Be humble because you are made of shit. Be noble because you are made of stardust.'

Ramesh says that this is his favorite passage from Lao Tzu:

> When everyone knows beauty as beautiful, there is already ugliness. When everyone knows good as goodness, there is already evil. To be and not to be arise mutually. Difficult and easy are mutually realized. Long and short are mutually contrasted. High and low are mutually posited. Before and after are under mutual sequence.

And he often quotes this passage, which is also from Lao Tzu:

> When the great Tao was lost, there came ideas of humanity and justice. When knowledge and cleverness arrived, there came great deceptions. When familiar relations went out of harmony, there came ideas of good parents and loyal children. When the nation fell into disorder and chaos, there came ideas of loyal ministers.

Tsing Sang, the Zen poet, has said, 'If you want to get to the plain truth, be not concerned with right and wrong. The conflict between right and wrong is the sickness of the mind.'

Ramesh also says, 'Love or compassion is that state which transcends the interconnected opposites of love and hate. And that is the state which is the impersonal state. It is the "me" which is concerned with the interconnected opposites and choosing between them.'

Ramesh quotes from the Ashtavaka Gita:

> Desire is at the root of ignorance, and so long as desire persists, the sense of the acceptable and the unacceptable — which is the branch and the sprout of the tree of samsara — must necessarily continue. Activity begets attachment. Abstention from activity generates aversion. Being rid of the bondage of opposites, the wise man, established in the Self, lives like a child. One who is attached to samsara wants to renounce it in order to free himself from misery. But one who is not attached continues to remain in samsara and yet lives happily. He who seeks enlightenment is an individual seeker and still is identified with the body, is neither a jnani nor a yogi, and suffers misery. Unless everything is totally forgotten, you cannot be established in the Self, even if Shiva or Vishnu or Rama be your preceptor. Whatever you hear is still a concept, whatever knowledge you acquire is still the opposite of ignorance.

'Duality is the basis of life itself, the total unconditional acceptance that there have always been Mother Teresas on one hand and psychopaths on the other — that life is based on interconnected opposites over which no human being can possibly have any control. Therefore, the opposites must exist – happiness and unhappiness – beginning with Adam and Eve:

> I've said Adam and Eve. Reminds me of a joke. When the Lord created Eve for Adam, Adam was delighted. So he thanked God for creating Eve for him. He said, 'But I want to know why did you make Eve so beautiful and so attractive?' And the Lord said, 'So that, my son, you may love her.' 'And why did you make her so considerate and eager to look after my welfare?' 'So that, my son, you may love her.' Then Adam said, 'But, Lord, why have you made her so stupid?' 'So that, my son, she may love you.'

The following illustration is one that Ramesh frequently uses, pointing out the natural acceptance of both creation and destruction in child's play:

> As I often say, take a child to the seashore and give the child a bucket and a spade, and stay there for awhile. The amount of time and trouble it takes to build a sandcastle is astonishing, especially if a lot of children get together. But when they are told, 'Let's go home,' they just kick it down. If the adult asks, 'Why did you build it and now demolish it?' The child honestly will think the adult is crazy and will answer, 'I liked to build the sandcastle, and I liked to destroy it.'

INTERRELATED OPPOSITES – PAIN, SUFFERING AND EVIL

When Ramesh is speaking on the topic of interrelated opposites (and often when he is speaking on some other subject), the questions about why there is pain and suffering and evil in the world get asked. Ramesh has noted that people do not ask him why there is pleasure and goodness and joy in the world! He comments that the human mind wants to eradicate what it does not like:

> Swami Nityananda was Swami Muktananda's guru. A woman friend of mine went to Swami Nityananda. She was a very sensitive person. She was worried about the terrible things happening in the world: starvation, fighting, people being killed, and so much unhappiness. She said that for families who were associated with Nityananda, he was God. So she asked him, 'Why is there so much unhappiness in the world?' His answer was very peculiar. He said, 'The postman delivers you your letters. The postman does not deliver to you somebody else's letters.'
>
> Ramana Maharshi's answer to the same question was, 'God created the world. Leave the problems of the world to God.'

'Many psychopaths – people who try to conquer the world like Hitler – say that they heard a voice from God . And who is to deny this? If they don't believe in God, they say, "I am a man of destiny" – like Napoleon. In Napoleon, this conviction that he was a man of destiny was so complete that his personality was based on it. When someone came to assassinate him with a knife, all he did with the greatest of conviction was look at the assassin probably thinking, "What can he do to me? I am a man of destiny." He looked at him and the man dropped the dagger and ran away. And when psychopathic people fall, as undoubtedly they must, the amount of feeling of degradation and frustration is enormous – Napoleon on the island of Elba, Hitler when he felt forced to commit suicide. Many psychopaths have testified in court in response to the question, "Why did you do it?" saying, "God commanded me to do it." Therefore, William Blake put it, **"These people have turned to God without first turning away from themselves."** And even that is part of the functioning of Totality, and precisely what they are supposed to do.'

INTERRELATED OPPOSITES – DEATH

'Until its first experience of death, a child takes life for granted. Its first experience of death brings into its mind the corresponding opposite of life':

> My granddaughter was probably three years old. She had not yet encountered death. Then someone died, and there was talk of death. So she asked my son, her father, 'What is death?' Some sort of explanation could have been given that would satisfy a child of three, but no, that was not the way my son was programmed. He said, 'The child must know.' And he started explaining in great detail what death was all about. My wife and I looked at each other. That's not the way we would have done it, but the child was his, not ours. So he explained beautifully to this extremely intelligent child. She heard the whole thing and finally she came out with this remark, 'Yes, Daddy, I understand what you say. But I am not going to die!' Deep down, intuitively, she knew that she wasn't born and she wasn't going to die.

'It's also instructive to consider what the sage says about the process of dying, which sometimes is feared because of the possibility of it being a painful one. The sage tells us that every dying person does not necessarily undergo great pain and agony. It would seem that those who are inordinately attached to the material world and all that it offers resist the process of death, and thereby create a conflict. And it is this conflict which is the cause of the pain and the agony in the process of death. On the other hand, there are those who accept death as a natural consequence of life and merely witness the process as they would witness any other event in life. And thus there is no conflict, but only a sense of floating through the process easily and smoothly':

> I was with friends at the golf course in the early morning when it was just dawning. We were on the fifth tee, just about to leave it when suddenly there came, almost as if to attack us, a bird of the family of eagles we call it a kite. Its wing span is enormous. It came straight at us as we left. Then this bird did a fantastic thing. It landed on the raised tee, facing the sun. It landed flat on its belly, spread its wings, raised its neck, looked at the morning sun, and laid its head down and died. One of the men said, 'Cashing in your chips, are you fellow?' His comment jarred my nerves. His was one way of looking at it. For me it was simply one of the most beautiful things I've ever seen. It was one of the most dignified events, the most amazing incidence of sheer dignity — his landing facing the sun, raising his neck and then lying down. The bird obviously knew it was dying. There was no panic at all. No fluttering of the wings or showing any signs of commotion or disturbance. A perfectly dignified exit from the scene.

Ramesh tells this story about his brother-in-law witnessing his own death, and several other stories about the lack of fear that can accompany the process of dying:

> When my brother-in-law died I wasn't present, but I was told the whole incident. He had lived one of the most regular lives: regular meals, regular long walks. And he was a doctor. However, he didn't want to practice because he felt that his success as a practicing

doctor would depend upon the illness of others. He didn't want to do that. So he took a comparatively small job with the municipality, a sort of government job, which limited his means. He had a wife and just one daughter who were perfectly willing to live a simple life, so life didn't present much problem to him. He was not interested in the path of knowledge; his was essentially a path of bhakti. He played the percussion instrument, the tabla, so he was in great demand where bhajans (devotional songs) were being sung. He loved doing that. So when I started going to Maharaj, (at that time he had retired also, we were almost the same age) whenever we met I would start talking about Maharaj. It became a sort of addiction. It was difficult to stop talking about him. In about five minutes I could see his mind wandering, so I said, 'You're not interested. Forget about it.' He was not really interested in the path of knowledge at all.

My brother-in-law was one of the people that I would say was the last possible candidate for a heart attack. Regular life, regular exercise, no problems in life as such; and suddenly one evening he had a very bad heart attack, an intensive heart attack, and he died. I was told about what happened when he was dying. He was a very popular man and he had a lot of friends who were doctors. The moment he had chest pains he telephoned a friend and in five minutes he came with his EKG instrument. The doctor was taking his cardiogram, and the doctor knew straightaway that it was only a matter of minutes. The cardiogram was showing basically a flat line. He himself was a doctor so he knew, too. His wife asked if they should go to the hospital — she was concerned with packing the overnight bag. He said, 'We'll wait and see.' He knew there was no question of his being taken anywhere, other than to the cremation ground.

This doctor who attended told me the next day about this astonishing process. He said, 'I saw it but I don't believe it.' He said my brother-in-law was telling him precisely what was happening in the process of death. He said, 'I have a numbness in my toes. The numbness is creeping up. The numbness is now in my knees.' He described the numbness until it reached his heart, and then he died with a smile on his lips. A perfect case of witnessing one's own death. He was not a jnani, but he did have the basic essential intuitive feeling of the impersonality of the process that is in this manifestation.

❋ ❋ ❋

The sage, Vishista — in Hindu mythology he was supposed to be the guru of Sri Rama — in an astonishingly perceptive small passage, gives his verdict on death. 'While no one really knows what happens after death, there are only two possibilities. Either the dead just cease to exist, or they exist in other bodies. Death would denote an exceedingly happy consummation if it means the total extinction of the one who is dead, because that would necessarily mean the end of all the vexatious restlessness of living and the freedom from all the ever-changing uncertainty of pains and pleasures of living. If, on the other hand, death means not the end of life, but merely a change of body, would it not be foolish to fear the phenomenon of death which provides them with a new body? Either way, why should we fear death.'

Our host in Santa Barbara, Dr. Ben Weininger, was extremely well known as the 'five-cent psychotherapist.' He said he got the idea from a comic strip called *Peanuts*. He wanted his services to be available to anyone who needed it. Lots and lots of people knew him and the whole area was full of his friends. He was that kind of a man. He was dying; there was no question about it. He knew it, his wife knew it, and yet they wanted me to be their guest during that week in Santa Barbara. We said we could easily make other arrangements, and his wife said, 'No, Ben wants it.' He did die during that week I was in Santa Barbara. Twenty-four hours before he died I had a long talk with him. He said, 'I want to have a talk with you. I'll be your first personal interview.' But the next morning he wasn't well enough. So it got postponed until just the day before he died. He was very weak. It was obvious it was just a matter of days, if not hours. So I sat by his bed and we talked. He talked and he dozed. When he woke up he said, 'Are you still here?' I said, 'Yes. I don't have to go anywhere.' So we talked some more, and he dozed some more and it went on like this for about an hour and a half. And it was so clear that it was doing him a lot of good. He was not afraid of death; that was clear enough. But somehow I think he wanted company in death; someone who understood the procedure of what was happening. So the fear of the unknown was probably there to a little extent, and my being there helped him.

※ ※ ※

Chuang Tzu, writing on the death of his master, Lao Tzu, said, 'The master came because it was time for him to come. He left because he followed the natural flow of events. Be content with each moment of eternity, and be willing to follow the flow. Then there will be no cause for joy or grief. In the old days this was called freedom from bondage. The wood is consumed but the fire burns on and we do not know when it will come to an end.'

※ ※ ※

Ramana Maharshi, when he was dying and people were weeping, said, 'Why are you weeping? I am not going anywhere.' And subsequently he added, 'I will always be here. Where can I go?'

ACCEPTANCE AND SURRENDER

Ramesh says that acceptance is more of a jnana process, and surrender is more of a bhakti process, and that dispassion is another term for the same two processes. 'They really mean living in the present moment without being attached to anything.' He has many stories that illustrate this point:

> **There was a saintly man, a Sufi. He lived his life quietly in his own small house. Then one of the neighboring young women got pregnant and she gave birth to a child. Everyone wanted to know who the father was. She didn't want to give up the name of her lover, so she gave the name of the Sufi. The community then insisted that the Sufi bring up the child. They came to him and he said, 'All right, leave the child.' He brought up the child with whatever means he had. Two or three years later, the mother relented and she was sorry. She and her lover got married and they confessed that the Sufi was not the father of the child. They went to the Sufi and said, 'We are very sorry that we made this mistake. Please give us the child back.' He said, 'Take it.'**

These two anecdotes of Ramana Maharshi's are examples of deep acceptance of whatever is going to occur:

> **Perhaps even more relevant and pertinent, and I would say shocking in modern times, is the answer given by Ramana Maharshi to a query put to him by a sincere young seeker. The seeker said, 'I am carried away by the sight of the breasts of a young woman neighbor and I am afraid of committing adultery with her.'**

He implored Ramana Maharshi, 'Please tell me what I should do.' The answer given by Ramana was amazingly straightforward. He said, 'You are always pure. It is your senses and body which tempt you, and which you confuse with your real self. So first know who is tempted and who is there to tempt. But even if adultery does take place, do not think about it afterwards because you yourself are always pure. You need not feel guilty. You are not the sinner.'

❋ ❋ ❋

Some robbers came into Ramana Maharshi's place and beat up many people including Ramana Maharshi. His comment was, 'You all worship me with flowers; they worship me with a stick. That is also a form of worship. If I accept yours, should I not accept theirs as well?'

The following stories continue the illustration of acceptance of the nature of things:

A Brahmin was having his bath in the river. Then he noticed a scorpion almost drowning. So he lifted the scorpion and put it on the ground. But before he could put it on the ground, the scorpion bit his hand. Many people were sitting around and some said to him, 'What have you achieved? You have spared him only to get yourself bitten.' His answer was, 'I did what I had to do according to my nature. The scorpion did what it had to do according to its nature.'

❋ ❋ ❋

A rabbi who had the Understanding lived in a tiny room with no stools to sit on and a desk which served as his bed at night. Anybody who came to see him had to sit on the ground or stand to talk. One of his visitors said, 'Rabbi, where is your furniture?' The rabbi said, 'Where is yours?' The visitor replied, 'I am only passing through.' The rabbi replied, 'So am I.'

This is a famous Zen story which Ramesh frequently quotes:

> A farmer lived in the days when fighting was going on between small kingdoms in China. This farmer had a son. His son, with the aid of the horse, was tilling a small field. One day the horse ran away. The neighbors came and said, 'It's a very bad thing. You have such bad luck.' The farmer said, 'Maybe.' So the next day the horse came back with half a dozen other wild horses. The neighbors came again and they said, 'What tremendous luck.' So he said, 'Maybe.' On the third day the son, while trying to ride one of the wild horses, fell and broke his leg. Again, the neighbors came and said what bad luck it was, and the farmer said, 'Maybe.' The next day the king's people came to recruit strong healthy farmers into the army. When they found this farmer's son with a broken leg they left him alone. So, again, the neighbors came and said it wasn't such bad luck after all and that everything had turned out well. The farmer said, again, 'Maybe.'

This metaphor is by Chuang Tzu, and is called 'The Empty Boat':

> He who rules men lives in confusion. He who is ruled by men lives in sorrow. The Tao therefore desires neither to influence others nor to be influenced by them. The way to get clear of confusion and free of sorrow is to live with Tao in the land of the great void. If a man is crossing a river and an empty boat collides with his own skiff, even though he be a bad-tempered man, he will not become very angry. But if he sees a

man in the boat he will shout at him to steer clear.
If the shout is not heard, he will shout again and yet
again, and begin cursing. Yet, if the boat were empty
he would not be shouting and not angry. If you can
empty your own boat, crossing the river of the world,
no one will oppose you. No one will seek to harm you.
He who can free himself from achievement and from
pain descends and is lost amid the masses of men. He
will flow like Tao, unseen. He will go about like life
itself, with no name and no home. Simple is he
without destination. To all appearances he is a fool.
His steps leave no trace. He has no power. He achieves
nothing. He has no reputation. Since he judges no one,
no one judges him. Such is the perfect man. His boat
is empty.

'Being unattached is quite different than being an ascetic,' Ramesh says about the following story:

King Janaka still worked as a king after enlightenment
happened. He did all his kingly duties, including the
pleasures and the entertainment that came with his
role. Once a guru had a disciple with a great deal of
understanding, but who put a great deal of importance
in asceticism. The guru sent the disciple to King
Janaka. The disciple arrived at King Janaka's court in
the evening and he found the king enjoying his usual
entertainment. There was a feast going on, girls
dancing, and everything that was expected of a king.
So this disciple said, 'Why has my guru sent me here?
This is just entertainment. King Janaka is enjoying all
this just like a rich man.' King Janaka said to him, 'Go
and rest for the night. In the morning at six o'clock I'll
pick you up and we'll go for a walk in the garden and
talk about things which your guru has asked you to

discuss with me.' So the next morning King Janaka picked up this disciple. As they started walking the disciple noticed a big fire in the quarters where he had spent the night. He said to the king, 'Your Majesty, there's a fire there.' The king said, 'Yes, yes, yes. Let's go on and talk.' They go a little further and the disciple says again, 'There is a fire there!' And the king says, 'Yes, yes. Let's talk.' The disciple takes a few more steps and then he couldn't wait any longer. So he said, 'Your majesty, you may have many clothes, but my only other loincloth is in there, hanging on a string and drying.'

SEEKING

'The seeking begins at a particular time, and it progresses in phenomenality until there is a breakthrough. I'm not saying that that breakthrough is the final breakthrough, but this process is a series of breakthroughs. So the whole process is the impersonal Consciousness, which has identified itself as a personal consciousness, seeking its own source. The seeking always begins with an individual, and the seeking ends with the annihilation of the individual.'

A point that Ramesh makes again and again is that you cannot escape from life into enlightenment. The following talk about samsara (personal reality) and nirvana (Self-realization or Enlightenment) illustrates this.

'Yesterday evening I mentioned Buddha's words, "Nirvana and samsara are not two, they are one." I am not a student of Buddhist religion; I don't know if the Buddha explained any more about this beautiful sentence, nor do I know if any subsequent interpretations have been made. But the way I interpret that sentence, "Nirvana and samsara are one," relates to the seeker who seeks nirvana as a place to escape into from the difficulties of samsara. The Buddha tells him you can't do it. They are not two. If you want to enjoy nirvana, you can do it only in samsara:

> **A friend of mine told me once that he, his father, and his father before him used to go to Bangalore to the Ramakrishna mission and see the swami regularly and talk to him. This friend of mine, a young man, somehow didn't feel inclined to go as regularly as he was supposed to. The swami of this particular ashram mentioned to my friend's father, 'I haven't seen your son for quite some time.' The father mentioned it to the son and said, 'Why don't you go and see him?'**

> So the son went and they talked for a while, and then my friend asked this swami, 'Swamiji, may I ask you a question? I hesitate to ask it, but it is asked in all sincerity. It may sound like an impertinent question, but it is not, I assure you.' The question was this: 'Swamiji, you have been in this or some other ashram, safe and secure, for twenty-five or thirty years. You are supposed to advise the ordinary man about his problems in life. If you had to go out into life without the protection of the ashram for six months, could you do it?' The swami was startled. He thought for a moment, and he said, 'No. I don't think I could do it.'

'So, very often, the spiritual counselors have no experience of life, and yet they tell you how to live your life. Therefore, my point is, you have to live your life in samsara and still find nirvana.'

I have seen at many of the talks that Ramesh gives, that seekers have a very difficult time with the idea of the personal self and Enlightenment. Ramesh frequently speaks to this issue, and the following anecdote is a good example of what he has to say:

> One of the early persons who came to me, many years ago, was an intense person and he said, 'Ramesh, I can't tell you how much I suffer, waiting for this expectation to occur.' So I said, 'My friend, just suppose that I can hand you over your enlightenment on a platter, saying, "This is it. You're enlightened now." Supposing you are now enlightened. What will you do with the rest of your life? You're enlightened. Will you shout from the rooftops, "I'm enlightened!" What will you do? You cannot do anything for this reason: When enlightenment happens you will not be there to enjoy enlightenment as you now think you will. Why do you want enlightenment? You want enlightenment because you think, "I will enjoy everything that life has to offer

me in this life." It has been said in books and by masters that enlightenment means bliss. So what the mind says is, "I've enjoyed every kind of happiness in this world, now I want to enjoy the bliss." But there is no bliss to be enjoyed by anybody. Because enlightenment means the total annihilation of the "me". So I always say if you have the choice, and you don't have the choice, but if you have the choice of seeking a million dollars or seeking enlightenment, choose the million dollars because then there will be someone to enjoy that million dollars.'

❋ ❋ ❋

A group of professors in theology met every week. At one of their meetings one of the professors in the group said, 'God came to me last night and offered me total knowledge or total pleasure. I, of course, jumped at this chance and said, 'Total knowledge.' So the others said, 'All right, now tell us, what is this total knowledge?' The professor said, 'It was the wrong choice.'

In Gut Schermau in 1999 Ramesh read the following passage, entitled 'The Current of the River' from the book *Illusions* by Richard Bach. He said he was very fond of it:

Once there lived a village of creatures along the bottom of a great crystal river. The current of the river swept silently over them all, young and old, rich and poor, good and evil, the current going its own way, going its own crystal self. Each creature, in its own manner, clung tightly to the twigs and rocks of the river bottom. For clinging was their way of life, and resisting the current, which each had learned from life. But one creature said at last, 'I'm tired of clinging.

Though I cannot see it with my eyes, I do trust that the current must know where it is going. I shall let go and let it take me where it will. Clinging, I shall die of boredom.' The other creatures laughed and said, 'Fool. Let go and the current that you worship will throw you, tumbled and smashed across the rocks. And you will die quicker than from boredom.' But that one heeded them not. And taking a deep breath did let go and was tumbled by the current across the rocks. Just in time, as the creature refused to cling, the current lifted him free from the bottom and he was bruised and hurt no more. And the creatures downstream, to whom he was a stranger, cried, 'See, a miracle. A creature like ourselves, yet he flies. A messiah has come to save us all.' And the one carried in the current said, 'I am no more a messiah than you. The river delights to lift us free if we only dare let go. Our true work is our voyage, this adventure.' But they all cried all the more, 'Savior! Savior!' — all the while clinging to the rocks. And when they looked again, he was gone and they were left alone making legends of a savior.

The following story illustrates how stuck people can get, and the unpredictability of what might unstick them:

In 1988 a man came to see me. Usually people ring up and ask to see me and I say yes. Usually they ask what time will suit me; so I say four o'clock in the evening. So I asked him, 'What time would you like to come? Would four o'clock suit you?' This was about seven o'clock in the morning. So he said, 'I would like to come now.' He was going out of Bombay to a Vipassana meditation center at one o'clock. So I said yes. This man came around seven thirty. When I opened the door and saw him, it was almost as if he were ready to attack me. There was violent earnestness in his eyes. I invited him in and he sat down. He didn't even lean back in his chair, he just sat there and started in. He said, 'I've been wandering about in India from March through April and May.' (He came to me in June and you couldn't choose worse months to travel in India.) He said he had been travelling by train, bus, and he'd walked a lot. Something made him feel that he had to come to India, so he came to India. He voiced a strong complaint. He said that he had made a terrible mistake in coming to India. He had visited any number of temples. Wherever he went he found priests with their hands open wanting gifts. He visited any number of ashrams, and what did he find? He found ochre-robed aides to the master spouting spiritual texts, which he himself had read since he had been at it for twelve years. They were merely parroting what he had already read. So he said, 'What have I come to India for?'

All this time I was just listening. He didn't give me a moment to say anything anyway. So I said, 'Excuse me,' and went and got a bottle of chilled water. He just emptied it so I went in and got another one. And that made him cool down, both literally and spiritually. So then he realized what he was doing. He said, 'Don't you have anything to tell me?' I said, 'Do you expect anything?' So when he said, 'Yes,' I said, 'First tell me what you are doing? What made you into a seeker?' So he said he was a very successful engineer when suddenly the thought struck him that he only had the one daughter who was well settled, so he didn't need to work. He wanted to find out what life was all about. Then I asked him, 'How did you happen to come to me? I have no ashram. I have no aides to spout and parrot spiritual truths.' He said it was curious. He had been to Ramanasramam and had sat in the meditation hall for awhile and then someone came and sat beside him. He said there were not many people, but this man came and sat beside him. He said that the moment that anyone came near him, he would start his obsessive complaint. He said that he did exactly to him what he did to me; he complained. This man listened very patiently and then asked him, 'Afterward, where are you going?' He said he was going to Bombay and from there he was going to this meditation retreat center. So this man said, 'If you are in Bombay, go and see Ramesh.' He gave him my name, address, and telephone number. I asked, 'Who was he?' He said, 'I don't know, but he had your telephone number.' To this day I don't know who sent him.

So he sat for a moment, and then I asked him, 'Would you believe me if I told you that if I asked you only one question, and you found an answer to that question, you will have found an answer to all your questions?' He said, 'No. I don't believe you.' I said, 'Let's have a crack at it. My question is — you said you were a perfectly happy, contented, almost prosperous engineer and you have been suffering the tortures of hell, certainly during the last three months. What turned you from a happy and contented engineer into a miserable seeker? Did you choose to be a seeker?' He just sat for a while, and then he said, 'What do you mean?' I said, 'Wouldn't you like to have a try at answering the question?' He said he didn't have the time he was going to a Vipassana center. I said, 'Perhaps the meditation will give you the answer.' He said he didn't think so because he had been doing it for twelve years. So I said, 'Who is doing the seeking? You think you are seeking and I am telling you that *you* are not the seeker. Something turned you into a seeker. In fact, something has used your body-mind organism for the seeking. So what is it that is seeking? It is certainly not you. Who are you? You are just a body to which a certain name has been given. Find out 'who' is the seeker? You are not the individual seeker. The seeking is an impersonal process that is happening.' We talked more, for about an hour and a half, and he said he would like to come again, but he didn't turn up again in India. He turned up at one of my talks in the U.S.A. He said the main reason he had come to see me was to explain why he hadn't seen me, not because he didn't want to, but because he fell ill.

He attended the talks. The moment I sat down he put his hand up and asked the same question. He was precisely where he was four months ago — the same question. So obviously he hadn't thought much on it. I gave him an answer and he asked another question and this went on back and forth, back and forth, for almost twenty minutes. The other people were getting restless. Someone said, 'Look, this can go on interminably. Why don't you just sit back quietly and listen to other questions and answers that will come?' He got very angry, and he said, 'If I am not wanted, I will go.' So I told him, 'It is not that you are not wanted, but perhaps there is something in that suggestion if you will sit quietly for a few minutes, and listen to the other questions and the answers.' So he did that, with a great amount of discomfort. But he did sit through. It just so happened that on that very morning the first book printed in America, *Experiencing the Teaching* arrived. He bought a copy. The next morning, again before anyone else could talk, he waved the book and said, 'For twelve years I've been wanting this. It's here now. All the answers are here, and it's not a big book.' So if the others hadn't seen him ranting and raving the previous day, they would have thought that the publisher had planted him! At the end of the session he was such a changed man. Apparently he needed to be prodded in a certain way, which the book did for him. He calmed down so much that my wife couldn't believe that he was the same man who had come earlier to Bombay.

'The only seeker is the Self, or Consciousness, or God, there is no individual seeker. Seeking is not in the individual's hands. **The most comforting words for "miserable seekers" are those of Ramana Maharshi who said, "Your head is already in the tiger's mouth"':**

> Ramana Maharshi also once said to a disciple who was in great distress, wanting to know his true nature, 'When you do understand, you will remember this incident, this frustration and your wanting to know with great amusement.'

❋ ❋ ❋

> Chuang Tzu said, 'Let hearing stop with the ears, and the mind stop with the thinking. Then the spirit is a void, embracing everything, and only the Tao includes the void.'

Ramesh said at one of the seminars in Maui, 'It is only when the mind is vacant that inspiration, grace, call it what you want, can come inside. But if the mind is already full, how can anything come inside?':

> At Maui, when we left the house, Ed [Nathanson] asked me, 'Are you ready to knock some sense into the

group?' So I said, 'I'm ready to knock some nonsense into the group provided they let their common sense out!'

❋ ❋ ❋

There is a story of a Zen master. A man who had much learning and had studied with many masters, went to see the master and said, 'I want to be your pupil.' The master said, 'Fine.' He brought a pot of tea and started pouring it into the cup that he had set before his guest. The cup was full and he still kept pouring. The cup was overflowing and he still kept pouring. The guest said, 'Master! The cup is overflowing!' The master said, 'Yes. It is like your mind now. Unless you empty it, there is nothing I can put into it.'

SELF-INQUIRY

Ramesh advocates no practices – which does not mean that he doesn't think they are necessary. He says that if they are, you will be drawn to them and you will do them. And when they are no longer necessary, they will fall away. There is one process that he does recommend. That is the process of Self-inquiry.

'The uniqueness of this teaching, which is based on Ramana Maharshi's Self-inquiry, lies in this sadhana [practice] which has to be done by the ego. It is the ego that will investigate actions that happen through that body-mind organism, which the ego has been saying are its actions. The practice lies in inquiring over a day, or a longer period of time, whether any action is one's own action, or not. The inquiry I am referring to is the investigation of any action that has happened through this body-mind organism, and to find out if that action was your action, or did it just happen? Can any action truly be called mine? Day after day, if it is found out by personal experience that one truly can not call any action his or her action, then the ego gets weaker and weaker. If no action is "mine", who is this "me"?':

> About two months ago there was a visitor who intended to come for ten days and was here for three months, and was thinking of renting a flat so he could be here for another six months. He is a famous singer who was now a monk in a Zen monastery. The effect of this Self-inquiry has made such an impact for him that the transformation was visible to others. When we were talking about this investigation, he said a remarkable thing. He said, 'Do you know, Ramesh, I started this investigation at the end of the very first day. I sat down and examined action after action that came to my mind, which I thought were "my" actions.

The very first day I had come to the conclusion that no action was my action.' He said, 'Ramesh, a curious thing happened. The very second day I did not have to wait until the end of the day. As the action happened, the unconscious investigation began, and as the action concluded, before another action or thought could come, there was this conviction, "That was not my action."' In his case it was quick, probably because of many years of this Zen tradition. Whatever it was, the investigation lasted only one day and the very next day the investigation came to a conclusion. That was in his case.

SADHANA

Sadhana is spiritual practice. Ramesh does not usually prescribe a spiritual practice. Seekers, however, are usually looking for ways to 'make Enlightenment happen', and there are many questions about spiritual practice. Ramesh says, 'The trouble about sadhana is that it tends to become an end in itself, and if it continues to remain a means, there is an end remaining. Therefore there is a "me" practicing sadhana, wanting something in duration – the annihilation of the "me". If those three factors are there – the me, the wanting, and duration the Ultimate Happening cannot happen':

> This is not a story, this is a fact. In 1987 in Hollywood, we were talking about sadhana. Someone said that he started meditating one hour at a time. And he asked me with great pride, 'Do you know how long I now practice meditation? Fourteen hours a day.' So all I could say was, 'That is wonderful.' From his point of view it was. But that was his aim, an end in itself. What his actual limit was I don't know. You can gather that I didn't have to ask him what he did for a living!

❋ ❋ ❋

> When I started playing golf, there were three of us, so we started taking lessons together. After a while I began to notice that the less I thought about those do's and don'ts when in actual play, the better I played. There was one among the three of us who loved to practice. When he started to play he was thinking of what he should and shouldn't do. His play was terrible, so he preferred to practice and not to play. His practice was much more enjoyable. So he'd say, 'Come and watch me practice.'

'There must be some power that sends you to do sadhana. So at the moment when you do sadhana, sadhana is right for you. And at a time when sadhana is not necessary any longer, something happens and the sadhana falls off. At that time when the sadhana falls away, if there is grace, you let it go. If the grace is not there, you hang onto the sadhana and suffer. So the process and the letting go itself are really not in the hands of the individual':

> A Sufi went through the whole gamut of sadhana and ultimately wrote a confession. He said, 'For twelve years I was the smith of my soul. I put it in the furnace of austerity and burned it in the fire of combat. I laid it on the anvil of reproach and smote it with the hammer of blame and guilt until I made a mirror of my soul. For five years I was the mirror of myself and was forever polishing that mirror with diverse acts of worship and piety. Then for a year I gazed in contemplation, and what did I see? I saw on my waist a girdle of vanity and pride and self-conceit and reliance on devotion and approbation of my work. I labored for five years more until that girdle of pride and vanity became worn out and I professed Islam anew. I looked and saw that all created things were already dead. I pronounced four prayers over them, and returned from the funeral of them all. And without inclusion of creatures, through God's help alone, I attained unto God.'

Ramesh says that any sadhana done earlier is rarely wasted. It is part of the process:

> I had a guru for twenty years before I was with Nisargadatta Maharaj. He was genuine, absolutely sincere. But in his case his ultimate understanding was that his life was being run by his guru. He started building an ashram. He told me once, 'My guru has

asked me to build an ashram where people could come, spend three or four or five days of their holidays, and have a place to stay where they could be fed.' That was his guru's order. So this was the traditional Indian guru. He didn't take me on as a disciple until he was satisfied that I was fit to be his disciple. There was the traditional formal ceremony of initiation. At that time my seeking was so intense that I distinctly remember that when I sat before him, and the initiation ceremony was in progress, I began to weep uncontrollably. At the end of it I think even he was impressed. He kept saying, 'It will happen. It will happen. Don't worry, it will happen.' But this shedding of tears was finished at that state. Later, when I went to Maharaj there were no tears.

But this first guru was the traditional Indian guru who when he takes on the responsibility of accepting and initiating the disciple, he also takes on the responsibility for his whole life. The disciple goes to the guru and tells him, 'My wife is ill.' He will say, 'All right. Tell your wife to fast on Thursdays, go to such and such a temple on Tuesdays and take such and such a medicine.' That was part of his understanding as a guru. The disciple would say, 'My son has lost his job.' He would say, 'You do this japa at least a thousand times a day, you fast on such and such a day, go to the temple...' and he would inquire afterwards. So a traditional guru accepted the responsibility for the life of his disciples.

My firmest possible conviction, ever since I could remember, is that my life has already been chalked up, and no power on earth can change it. How much physical pain I am to bear, how much psychological pain I am to bear, how much pleasure I am going to have is all decided. Therefore, quite frankly, I didn't need my guru to assure my promotions. To that extent, very soon I came to the conclusion that while the theoretical teachings were wonderful, and I benefitted a lot from them, he was not my real guru. But as it was the nature of this body-mind organism not to leave, I didn't cut off the relationship. It went on for twenty years.

Ultimately I realized why it was destined to continue on for twenty years. It so turned out that people, especially two of them, went and encouraged my guru to build the ashram and promised him the money. They said, 'We know a lot of influential people; we will get you all the money you need. Go ahead and borrow it now from disciples on a no-interest basis and we'll pay you.' So, my guru, depending on them, borrowed the money from the disciples, who themselves needed the money, with the understanding that it would be repaid in one or two years. So the disciples could afford to give up the interest, but they needed their money back. They were middle-class families. And then later these two men came and said, 'We're very sorry. We can not get you the money.' And my guru was in a terrible financial state. Somehow it was the destiny of this body-mind organism to find out a way to get him out of this situation. To the end of his days, whenever he met me, he would remember and he would say, 'I don't know what I would have done if you were not there in the ashram with me then.' So, I continued for twenty years because I was supposed to bring help to my guru when he needed it.

My point is that I knew within a very short time that he was not my real guru. When I went to Nisargadatta Maharaj, the very first day, I said, 'I'm home. Now I'm home.'

One of the practices that my earlier guru had asked me to do was to visit a particular temple on Thursday mornings, which I was doing faithfully when I was in Bombay. When I started going to Maharaj I continued to go on Thursday mornings and from that temple I would visit Maharaj direct. One day at the temple the ceremony began later than usual. And it kept me from leaving at my usual time. So I stayed on. It made me about ten minutes later than usual. But I hurried out, got into a cab, and went to Maharaj.

The scheduled time was ten o'clock. I used to be there normally at quarter to ten. Jnani or not, Maharaj's natural temperament as a body-mind organism was impatience. Where could the impatience go? So I found him looking impatiently down the stairs to see whether I was coming or not. When I came he was obviously relieved. He said, 'You are late.' I said, 'No, Maharaj. Instead of being fifteen minutes early I am only five minutes early.' He said, 'What do you have in your hand?' What I had in my hand was the packet of prasad which the priest had given me. I was late and didn't realize that I still had the packet in my hand. Normally I would have put it in my pocket. So I told him, 'That is the prasad from the temple which I have been visiting for twenty years.' It did strike me then that Maharaj might say, 'You've been coming here for six months and you still visit temples?' But no, on the contrary, he said, 'Continue to do it until the need is no longer felt.'

The following Thursday I had to go out of town to visit my daughter in Bangalore. So I was away for two Thursdays. After I was back it rained so heavily that the roads were flooded and I could not have gone either to the temple or to Maharaj's. But the mind said,

'Well, you are justified. How could you go? You couldn't have gone anyway.' But the following Thursday I got ready to go. I had my shower and got ready, and then I found that it was ten minutes too early, so I just sat there. While I sat there the thought came to me, 'Why go to the temple?' I didn't go. I changed my clothes and went about my normal business.

There is a photograph of this presiding deity in my puja room. That deity was the original guru of this particular sect, of which my earlier guru was the fourth or fifth successor. This photograph was more than one hundred years old. This original guru had a fierce gaze, something like that of Maharaj's. That photograph just glared at you. So, on Friday morning when I went to the puja room, I had the thought, 'Now Swami will be even more ferocious this morning.' But when I bowed down and looked at the photograph, for the first time I noticed that instead of a glare there was almost a smile on his face, which meant, 'Now, you damn fool, now you know!'

'Those who can get something out of the seminar are only those who have come here empty. If there is some receptivity, then they can get something. Ramana Maharshi often remarked, **"The grace is always there, it depends on what receptivity you go there with."** He would say, **"The ocean is always there, if you want to take some water away it depends on how big the vessel is that you bring"**':

The disciple asked the master, 'What is the Buddha nature?' The master answered, 'The "mind" is the Buddha nature.' Some time later the disciple heard a more senior disciple ask the master the same question, 'What is the Buddha nature?' And the master answered, '"No mind" is the Buddha nature.' The disciple was confused and asked the master for an explanation. The master answered, 'When the baby is crying, I stop his crying with the answer "mind" is the Buddha nature. After the baby has stopped crying my answer is "no mind" is the Buddha nature.'

Ramesh gives excellent advice about how to attend to the words and teachings of any guru:

> Out of a group of three or four people, one rang me up and said, 'We are going to Krishnamurti's talks,' (this happened to be his last series of talks in Bombay) and he said, 'After that, can we come and see you?' I said, 'Yes, certainly.' When Krishnamurti's talks were over, they came and we talked the usual way. At the end of a couple of hours, they got up and said, 'We really have learned a lot here,' and they started to leave. One of them hesitated. Then he came back. He said, 'One final question. Why is it that we have attended Krishnamurti's talks for thirty years, and yet in two hours now, the picture is so much clearer?' He hesitated because he didn't want to be disloyal to Krishnamurti. So I said, 'The answer is simple. Maharaj's teaching begins where Krishnamurti ends. Krishnamurti talks to the individual. He explains the situation, but nonetheless he talks to the individual. Maharaj's begins with saying, "There is no such thing as the ego. Where is the ego? Produce it and I'll slay it." Mind you, I have the greatest respect for Krishnamurti, but when you listen to him, listen totally. When you read him, read totally. But after that, think, meditate on what you have heard. Find out if it is acceptable, and if there are a few doubts, get them cleared, and then stay in it. Krishnamurti

talks like any other. If what Krishnamurti says has been meditated upon then most of this confusion will go. If there is true meditation, if you really go into what he is saying beyond his words and beneath his words, almost certainly you will come to the conclusion which you have just taken.'

The following are two more anecdotes about the relationship between Ramesh and Nisargadatta Maharaj regarding sadhana:

> Maharaj had a very pliant attitude. He, himself, was not a vegetarian. He had meat once or twice a week, but that didn't mean that his disciples had to be non-vegetarians. He smoked, but that didn't mean all his disciples had to be smokers. But that is how the human mind takes it — 'What Maharaj did I should do so I shall be what Maharaj was.' Wrong! Maharaj asked me once, 'Do you eat meat?' I said, 'Maharaj, I eat whatever comes to my table. I don't like certain things; I don't like red meat but I eat what comes to my table and I drink what comes to my table.' He gave me a big grin.

❋ ❋ ❋

> Maharaj asked me once when I first went to him, 'Do you meditate?' I said, 'Yes, Maharaj, my earlier guru asked me to meditate, but I was so busy traveling a lot that I was not able to meditate regularly. But whenever I can, I do meditate, maybe a half an hour, an hour.' He said, 'Good.' Then later after about six months he asked me, 'How is your meditation getting along?' So I said, 'Maharaj, I didn't give a thought to it. But, now that you ask, I find that I do not sit regularly in meditation.' At that moment I thought he would get very angry, but instead he remarked jokingly, 'Oh, you

don't think there is a need for you to meditate now that you are a big jnani!' I replied, 'It is astonishing that meditation happens more often than previously, and it just happens and I like it.' Maharaj said, 'Excellent.' So, meditation is necessary up to a certain point, but to make a fetish of that meditation is a different thing altogether.

This story was told in a seminar in Germany, where each talk was followed by the singing of bhajans to the accompaniment of a single guitar:

> If you like to sing bhajans, sing bhajans. If you don't like to sing bhajans, when bhajans start here, you walk out. At Maharaj's place in the evenings, bhajans used to be sung, but they were not like this. They were the traditional Hindu bhajans with eight or ten people shouting at the top of their voices, bells banging, and cymbals — enormous noise. And the very first time I was there Maharaj noticed I couldn't bear it. (I normally didn't go in the evening.) Maharaj once asked, 'You don't go in the evenings?' So I said, 'Morning session is enough for me for the twenty-four hours. I wouldn't be able to digest another session in the evening.' Which was true. So once Maharaj said that the translator in the evening might not be able to come. Would I come? I said, 'Certainly, with pleasure.' So I went and it so happened that the evening translator was there so I didn't have to do anything. Then the talk was over and the bhajans started. Maharaj looked at me and he made a gesture I could leave.

Ramesh says, 'The danger of most sadhana and I'm not saying it happens every time, is that the ego prides itself on its discipline and gets stronger and stronger.'

SADHANA — PRAYER

To pray sincerely is difficult. To become a priest who leads a prayer is easy. It is like total surrender to the Divine, which is truly what a prayer is, without which the Divine cannot enter. Without the sincere surrender, the necessary emptiness is not there. In the words of Soren Kierkegaard, 'In the beginning when I started to pray, I used to talk much to God. Then, by and by, I came to the understanding of what foolishness I was doing. I was talking. How can talking be prayer? Prayer can only be a deep listening, not a talking. You have to be silent so God can be heard. You have to be so silent that the silent and still word of God can penetrate you. In that silence, the Divine is revealed. You have to be passive, yet alert, open, and totally receptive. Otherwise your prayer in words is a waste of time and energy. Prayer is not of the mind, it is entirely of the heart. Words are not only unnecessary, they are a hindrance. A prayer cannot be effective unless there is the deepest conviction "I am nobody, I am helpless." The effectiveness of the prayer does not depend on, the intensity with which you beg, but on the depth of the openness with which you pray. The only real prayer is, "Thy will be done." When the mind is not working, you are in prayer.'

❋ ❋ ❋

There is an old Leo Tolstoy story about three people living on an island. They are perfectly simple people. A priest visits that island and gives these three people a long prayer. They try to remember it but they can't. The priest has returned to his ship and is sailing away from the island. He sees the three people coming towards him, running over the water. When they get to the ship they say, 'We're sorry. Before you leave, tell us the prayer again. We haven't quite got it.' The priest could only say, 'For you no prayer is necessary.'

❋ ❋ ❋

Repeating God's name, is technically called japa, or mantra. There is an ashram in the south of India where to this day, at the end of the day, a person sits at a desk and each person attached to the ashram lines up and tells him how many times the japa was repeated. And someone adds them up for the day. And ultimately what happens, I don't know. The ego says, 'I have done japa five hundred thousand times today. Last month I was able to do only three hundred thousand, so I must be getting closer to Self-realization.' So the danger with this sadhana is that the ego may get stronger.

SADHANA — ASCETICISM AND DENIAL

It is easy for pride and attachment to become associated with the very sadhana that one practices with the intent of loosening such attachments. The following anecdotes illustrate this point:

> Diogenes, the famous cynic philosopher, argued that to be happy one must rid himself of all riches, honors, powers, and all the enjoyments of life. And he practiced what he preached, going barefoot through Athens, never wearing a coat, eating coarse foods, and inveighing against corruption and comfort. Diogenes was, in fact, convinced of his superiority and did not hesitate to abuse those who disagreed with him. It is reported that Socrates once said to him, 'I see your vanity through the holes in your garments.' Even more telling is the incident of Diogene's visit to Plato in his home. When the cynic walked across Plato's beautifully and richly carpeted floors, he stopped, glared at his host stamped his foot squarely on the carpet, and said, 'Thus do I tread on the pride of Plato.' 'Yes,' said Plato, 'And with a greater pride.'

❉ ❉ ❉

> Lao Tzu chided Confucius for his moralizing. He said, 'All this talk of goodness and duty, these perpetual pinpricks, unnerve and irritate the hearer. You had best study how it is that heaven and earth maintain their eternal course, that the sun and moon maintain their light, and the stars their serried ranks, the birds and beasts their flocks, the trees and shrubs their station. This, too, you should learn to guide your steps

by inward power to follow the course that nature sets. And soon you will no longer need to go around laboriously advertising goodness and duty. The swan does not need a daily bath in order to remain white.'

The following passage might easily be misunderstood without its context. It was given as advice to disciples who had been frustrated with the futility of religious fasting and other disciplinary practices:

Let the ear hear what it longs to hear. The eye see what it longs to see. The nose smell what it likes to smell. The mouth speak what it wants to speak. Let the body have every comfort that it craves. Let the mind do as it will. What the ear wants to hear is music, and to deprive it of this is to cramp the sense of hearing. What the eye wants to see is eternal beauty, and to deprive it of this is to cramp the sense of sight. What the nose craves for is to have near it the fragrant plants, and if it cannot have them, the sense of smell is cramped. What the mouth desires is to speak of what is true and what is false. If it may not speak, then the knowledge is cramped. What the body desires for comfort is warmth and good food. Thwart its attainment of these, and you cramp what is natural and essential for man. What the mind wants is liberty to stray whither it will, and if it has not this freedom, the very nature of man is cramped and thwarted.

This joke is on the same subject of renunciation:

A millionaire became an ardent spiritual seeker. He rang up some swami's home that was suggested to him and said, 'Swami. I am a millionaire. Now I've turned my attention to spiritual seeking, and I'm told that my greatest obstacle is my attachment to money. What should I do?' The swami said, 'Just don't do anything! Wait until I come and see you.'

* * *

A friend of mine, connected to the best known (or it could be the other way around) ashram in India for the last twenty-five years, told me that he had given in all a donation of $1,000,000 less $25,000. And then he got so disgusted that he left the ashram and left everything there. So this happens also.

SADHANA – RITUAL

'A symbol is just a symbol, and one tends to forget that. The intellect sees the symbol as something in its own right. That's the trouble with any symbol, any practice, any ritual':

> An ashram had a cat, and when the ashram rituals began the cat used to come and disturb the proceedings. The head of the ashram suggested that a basket be put on the cat, so it was done. In the course of time it became a ritual. So when the ashram had no cat, the ashram had to borrow one to put the basket on.

THE GURU-DISCIPLE RELATIONSHIP

'Basically the Eastern concept of the guru-disciple relationship is this: It is the coming together of two body-mind organisms as part of the functioning of the manifestation. The coming together is the destiny of the two body-mind organisms, and is part of something that is supposed to happen':

> Ramana Maharshi put that very easily. He said, 'What the guru does is to push the understanding from the talk to within. And the Self within pulls this understanding into Itself.' So whatever the guru does is an outside event. But truly Consciousness speaks to Consciousness.

✻ ✻ ✻

> In *Thus Spake Zarathustra* by Fredrick Nietzche, Zarathustra gives his disciples the ultimate message. 'Whatever had to be said has been said. Whatever had to be understood has been understood. Now forget whatever has been said. Forget everything I've said except this last message: Beware of Zarathustra.' (So, beware of Ramesh!)

In answer to the question, 'Does everyone need a guru?', Ramesh gave the following reply:

> Ramana Maharshi suddenly had a feeling that his body was going to die and so he didn't send for a doctor. Instead he thought, 'Let me watch what happens.' He lay down and really got into the situation. 'Now the body is dead; the body is hard; the body is being taken

to be cremated; the body is now being burned.' He concluded, 'In all that there is a witness that is not concerned with the body.' And then it dawned on him that he is not the body, he is that witness — that which is witnessing the whole process. So he didn't need a guru. And yet when that happened someone mentioned the word Arunachala, and it rang a bell. It rang a bell so loudly that he gave up everything. His brother had given him money for school books. He took the money and went to the station and said, 'Which is the next train?' The ticket master said, 'Where do you want to go?' He replied, 'Wherever this money will take me.' So he gave him a ticket that happened to go to Arunachala. So that body-mind organism did not need a guru. But he's a rare exception.

Ramesh is non-traditional about the guru-disciple relationship. He does not require loyalty from the people who come to him. He told a story about a lady who came to see him in the desert of southern California when he first came to the United States to give some talks:

> She came to me and said, 'There is a master in the East Coast whom I went and found. I'm extremely attracted to him, and I want to go to him.' I said, 'What prevents you? By all means go. When you go you need have no qualms about loyalty or disloyalty to any teacher. But it may happen that after awhile you want to leave. Then leave, by all means, without any feelings of guilt.'

'Maharaj understood that the guru does not have to parrot his guru, and that teaching, if it is meant to happen, will happen spontaneously once the Understanding is complete:

At one point Maharaj was talking to me and he said, 'Many of my brother disciples do not agree with what I am saying. Their objection is that I do not say what my guru said. They themselves repeat as closely as possible what the guru was saying. I am not saying anything. Whatever I say comes out and that is what my listeners need. And, therefore, what comes out has nothing to do with the words or the way that my guru taught. But the teaching is still the same; it cannot be anything else.' And then he added, 'When you talk (at that moment I had no intention at all of talking to anybody — I did not like to talk — I hated talking) you will not be saying what I am saying. What you say will be totally different. The teaching is still the same but what you say will be different; what you say will depend on what your listeners need.'

BHAKTI AND JNANA

In India there are three paths to Enlightenment, Awakening, or Total Understanding. One is bhakti, which is a path of the heart, of worship and devotion. Another is jnana, or knowledge, which is Taoism or the Advaitic way. The third is karma, or the path of service to others. Ramesh says that the bhakti and jnana paths lead to the same goal:

> When we arrived in Santa Barbara there was a request from someone who said that he would try to attend the talks if possible, but he would very much appreciate a personal interview being set up. He was going to fly into Santa Barbara in his own plane, and after the interview was over, he might have to go back right away. He was coming out, I think from Sedona, just for this interview; so it was extremely important to him. When he said he was flying his own plane, I imagined some comparatively young man. The man who turned up was in his early eighties. He had a young woman with him who probably piloted the plane, or he may have piloted it himself.
>
> The man's big problem, and it really was a problem, was this. He had met Ramana Maharshi a few years before he died, and he said that that meeting with Ramana Maharshi produced such an impact that it changed his whole life. Thereafter, he considered himself a follower, a devotee of Ramana Maharshi's teachings, which he understood as the pure path of knowledge, although Ramana Maharshi repeatedly said that there is no difference between devotion and knowledge. Nonetheless, he had misunderstood the teaching, and he thought that devotion was something

not meant for someone at his level who had deeply imbibed Ramana Maharshi's teaching.

So his big problem was this. There was a woman saint who at that time was in the area, and someone had written to him and asked if he would host her visit to his part of the country. He said he was not so inclined, and what he wanted to do was to refuse it outright. But before he could do that he had to leave on some business and he found that when he came back this saint was firmly established in his place with her retinue. So, being the gentleman that he was, he accepted the situation, and when he attended her talks and bhajans — these bhajans attracted him very much — he became wholly involved and that was his problem. He felt he was being disloyal to Ramana Maharshi.

He said, 'I'm still attracted to Ramana's teaching. What do I do?' As he was narrating this, tears flowed freely from his eyes. It just showed to what extent the problem really bothered him. So I told him, 'Whatever is happening, don't resist it. If you feel attracted, that attraction is there; the whole episode may be there to teach you something you need to know.' So he said, 'You mean I can go on?' I said, 'Of course.' He was so relieved. Then he said, 'But Ramana Maharshi?' I said, 'Ramana Maharshi can take care of himself. Don't you worry about Ramana Maharshi. By all means, enjoy this experience; enjoy this devotion that is being thrust on you. Enjoy it! But, there is just one thing. If after a while this attraction wears off, then let it wear off. Don't feel guilty about it. There is no need to feel guilty now because you are attracted, and there will be no reason to feel guilty when this devotion wears off. All you do is just go with the flow. Enjoy the devotion when it is there and, as I said, perhaps this is just to show you that devotion and knowledge are not two separate paths which is what Ramana Maharshi repeatedly said.' So he was one delighted man when he went back. I never met him afterwards, but I continued to correspond with him until he died a few years later.

❊ ❊ ❊

In the *Bhagavad Gita* there is a verse which in a way gives a higher value to jnana than bhakti. In that verse Lord Krishna says, 'When the bhakti for me, when the love for me, reaches a certain intensity, I bestow the power to receive — the jnana.' When the devotion reaches a certain stage I endow a certain receptivity to that person to receive knowledge.

❊ ❊ ❊

There is a curious story about possibly the most well-known bhakta in Maharashta — a person called Tukaram, who lived probably about 300 years ago. He was the most beloved saint in Maharashta. He was truly a bhakta. He has written more than five thousand verses. In the earlier verses he would pray to God — his personalized god, Vitala, an aspect of Lord Krishna. He said, 'Vitala, for the jnani you will make yourself understood in your impersonality; but for me, life after life, please be in your personal form so I can worship you.' Then, when the Knowledge happened, the same Tukaram tells his God, 'You are a cheat. You know that you and I are no different, yet you made me worship you for all these years.' He also writes in another verse, 'You foolish people. Why do you go to temples? Why don't you worship the God within?'

Maharaj himself said his 'pinda' — the real core of his being — was bhakti. He used to go to a temple and sing bhajans every evening until That power pushed him towards a guru who dealt with non-duality. But bhakti was his original nature. One day a group of disciples on Mahashivaratri day, went to a Shiva temple. At the temple was the inner sanctorum. They went there and there was a Shiva lingum. Somebody said, assuming an air of great piety, 'This Shiva lingum must be very, very sacred.' Maharaj replied, 'Yes, it is sacred enough for me to piss on.' (And this is from a bhakta!)

Ramesh says that bhakti and jnana are really the same thing. 'Ramana Maharshi's concept is that there are two ways to meet the summit. That is his concept. My own concept is different; there are not two ways — they are the same way. It begins with bhakti, "Thy will be done," and ends with jnana. Jnana happens when the illusion is noticed as an illusion, and the Source answers, "My dear child, there never was any "you" to suffer."'

AWAKENING

'Enlightenment means, in plain terms, understanding what is real and what is unreal':

> A friend of Maharaj's, who used to go to a certain jnani, forced him to go with him. The friend said, 'You must come.' Maharaj said he was practically dragged to the guru — he didn't even purchase the traditional garland of flowers, his friend purchased it for him. But once he was there at the very first talk, when the very first thing the guru said, something fantastic happened. His heart opened up. The guru had said 'You are not what you appear to be. You are the essence, which is unseen. What you appear to be is only a reflection, an objective expression of that Subject.' Maharaj said, 'When I heard that, everything opened up. I had no problems. I had no doubts. I had no troubles.' His guru was not in Bombay so he said he used to see his guru two or three or four times a year. After three or four years his guru died. But he said he didn't really need to see him any more. The very first time — It grabbed hold of him. He said he thought his original natural tendency was bhakti. Ever since he was a child he used to go to the temple and sing bhajans. Only he hadn't realized that that was only his superficial tendency. Knowledge was his real nature.

This quote is from the *Ashtavakra Gita*:

> It means bondage when the mind desires something or grieves at something. It means liberation when the

mind does not desire or grieve, does not reject or accept, does not feel happy or unhappy.

❈ ❈ ❈

Swami Vivekenanda's guru was essentially a bhakta. A story is told that his guru had the perspicacity — the inherent intuitive knowledge — that Vivekenanda's real nature was knowledge (although it was bhakti which had drawn him to his guru Ramakrishna Paramahansa). Ramakrishna pulled out a copy of the *Ashtavakra Gita* from under his pillow and said, 'Read this out to me.' When Vivekenanda read the first few stanzas he said, 'This is sacrilege! I won't read any further. It says, "I am God." How can that be? I won't read it.' So Ramakrishna said, 'All right. Don't read it for yourself. Read it for me.' And as the reading progressed, there was no longer any 'Vivekenanda' left. Although the guru's natural tendency was bhakti, he could recognize that in his disciple it was jnana.

❈ ❈ ❈

There is a famous story of Lao Tzu and his disciple. This disciple came to him with his face shining with the glory of achievement. He came to the master's feet and he said, 'Master, I've arrived.' So Lao Tzu sympathetically, compassionately put his hands on his shoulders and said, 'My son, you have not.' The disciple went away dejected. He came back some time later. This time there was no sense of achievement; there was only peace. He said, 'Master, It has happened.' So Lao Tzu asked him what had happened in the meantime. The disciple said, 'I accepted two things. I accepted your words that I had not arrived, that Enlightenment had not happened. Also, I knew for a fact that I had done everything possible that I could have done; that there was nothing more I could do. This I knew. So from then on I just went on about my business, forgetting about Enlightenment altogether. So while going about my business there was the sudden realization that there was nothing to be sought; that what I had been seeking was there already.'

❋ ❋ ❋

There is a very beautiful tale about an old woman who was quite close to Enlightenment. She goes in the moonlight to get some water in an earthen pot. As she comes out she misses her step and she stumbles and the pot falls. Then she suddenly realizes there is no pot, there is no water, there is no moon. So for that body-mind organism that event was the apparent reason for Awakening to happen.

A SAGE'S REALITY

Ramesh is asked many questions, again and again, about what his perception, his sense of reality, and what the daily details of his life are like. People are trying to get a sense of what it is like to live as an enlightened being, and it is clear from those questions that there are many misconceptions. Ramesh welcomes these questions and responds to them, often with great humor.

'There is no need to fear a jnani. He sees exactly as you see. If there are ten different people he sees them as ten different forms and shapes. But what he knows is that in those ten different shapes what functions is the same Consciousness. The differences are seen as differences, but what is seen at the same time is the unity in diversity. Suppose that you have ten different photographs of yourself taken in ten different costumes, including a woman's dress. For anybody who sees them they'll see ten different people, not only ten different costumes, but ten different people. But, you'll know it is the same person. So what the jnani knows is that all these appearances are different, but what functions in those appearances is the same Unity – which the ordinary person doesn't know':

> **Someone asked me, 'How do you spend your time?' I said, 'What time? When I'm hungry, I eat. When I'm thirsty, I drink. I take a drink of water, or whatever is available. When I feel like walking, I walk about in my apartment. And when there are people who want to talk, I talk. In other words, life is amazingly simple.'**

'Basically, apart from this witnessing and nonwitnessing, the underlying fact that I have noticed with enlightenment is that there are no expectations and no wants, which creates a sense of peace – waiting for whatever is to happen to happen. That does not mean thoughts of expectations don't arise. They arise. The curious part of it is that many of them do get satisfied. Whenever such a thing happens, a tremendous surge of gratitude arises':

> When I was in Hollywood the second year with my wife, early one morning I was getting ready for the talks. When traveling I would carry a small photograph of Ramana Maharshi. So I mentioned to her, 'I don't have a very good photograph of Ramana Maharshi. When I go back to Bombay I'll arrange for a reasonably large photograph of him to hang over my desk.' The same day after about half an hour, when I was ready for my talks, someone knocks on the door and comes in. He has a nicely framed photograph of Ramana Maharshi, just the size I would have bought. He says, 'I don't know why, but I thought you might like this.' I said, 'I do indeed.' And that photograph that came to me in 1988, eleven years ago, hangs over my desk now. I have plenty of photographs all over the place, so I say, 'That is the Hollywood Ramana.'

Ramesh says about donations, that they really have nothing to do with the need to receive. 'The basis of donations from visitors is as a token of the impact that the teaching has had on them. To that extent the need to give donations is the need to give, and the need to give does not depend on the need to receive. Sometimes it happens that what comes in, comes in when it is needed':

> Many times donations come. Once especially, I remember, my wife was in the hospital. A gentleman from Spain came, and I had seen him three or four times earlier. He was an extremely nice man, always with a smiling face. He knocks on the door, walks in and says, 'Ramesh, I understand your wife is in the hospital in the intensive care unit, which I know is very expensive. So, perhaps you can use this.' He puts

his hand out and there were five bundles of one-hundred dollar notes, which I counted later and it was $3,500. He just came in and gave it just like that. That he was wealthy enough to afford it goes without saying. And the donation did come when I needed it.

'The point is that there are no expectations and no wants. Because of *whose* destiny does the money come in? Not ours; we have only a few years to live. So obviously the money comes in because it is the destiny of my children and grandchildren, to whom the money will go – and some of the charities to which money regularly goes. So donations come and they flow':

> When my wife was in the hospital she knew it was extremely expensive, and it was extremely expensive. And yet it was paid without much problem. As the bills came the money was there. When she was well enough to ask – she couldn't speak because there was a tube in her mouth – she asked me. (Here, Ramesh makes a gesture of rubbing his forefinger against his thumb – the symbol for money.) I said, 'All the debts have been paid.' So she makes another gesture (a sweeping gesture) – money comes in and money goes out.

Ramesh spoke further on the nature of donations:

> As far as my guru, Nisargadatta Maharaj, was concerned, he had a very simple formula where donations were concerned, which I also follow. His formula was, 'I expect nothing. I demand nothing. I refuse nothing.'

❋ ❋ ❋

About Nisargadatta Maharaj, let me tell you an incident. One morning among the visitors was a Brahmin priest, sitting there with just a longhi (a piece of cloth covering his loins), a shirt, and a towel over his shoulder. His story was that he came from Ramana Maharshi's ashram. He didn't have any money. So he had gone to the train station and had gotten on the platform. As soon as the train arrived he got into it. After awhile when the ticket collector found that he had no money, he was thrown off the train. So he sat on that platform until the next train arrived. In this way it had taken him about forty-eight hours to get from Tiruvannamalai to Bombay.

He was a Brahmin priest, which could be seen. There have always been people in India who, seeing a Brahmin priest, offer him a meal. So that's how he got his meals. Yet Maharaj was concerned. He asked him, 'What accommodations have you made in Bombay?' He said, 'None. I'm just here and I couldn't wait to see you. I had the inspiration in Ramanasramam. Immediately I started and here I am.' There were eight or ten people there, most of them Indians, and Maharaj asked, 'Surely one of you can offer him a piece of floor where he can lie down.' Someone took him in and also fed him. And being a Brahmin priest, people employed him to do pujas. At the end of the month, he came to Maharaj and said, 'Maharaj, I'm leaving tomorrow. I can't tell you how happy I've been this month in Bombay, and listening to your talks. Please accept this small gift from me which I have earned doing pujas during this month.' And he presented Maharaj with one ten-rupee note.

A ten-rupee note, even in Maharaj's style of living, was a small amount. However, Maharaj accepted it with great dignity, as if it were a hundred times the amount. He put it, as usual, in his pocket and said, 'Thank you very much. When are you leaving in the morning?' He said, 'I'll come here and after the talk

I'll go.' After he left Maharaj sent his assistant to the tailor and got a new set of south Indian clothes for the Brahmin. When he came the next morning he formally presented the package and added one hundred rupees, and said, 'Please accept this from me.' It was such a wonderful gesture and that was the way he was.

Another way that Ramesh explains the sage's reality is by saying, 'The sage lives in duality; the ordinary man lives in dualism. Dualism means choosing; accepting duality is attainment':

> Ramana Maharshi describes the ego that still arises in the awakened sage as like the remnants of a burned rope. Athrough the rope is burned, the form of the rope remains, but you can't tie up anybody with that rope.

Ramesh gets asked many questions at some seminars, the majority of which are about what it's like to be 'Enlightened'. Ramesh accepts this label, but prefers to talk in terms of the Total Understanding having happened. As he says, 'There is no *one* to get enlightened.' He speaks quite frankly about his life, saying 'I've had my share of grief and I've had my share of pain':

> My elder son, Ajit, had asthma from a very early age. It began with eczema, a skin problem. We were warned that if the eczema were treated it might convert itself into asthma. The eczema was so bad that my wife and I decided we would have to take a chance, and we had the eczema treated. And, as we were warned, he got asthma. My wife and I have a very nice apartment, which was nicer fifty years ago. At that time we had a veranda open to the stars. So night after night, alternately, my wife and I would take this child on our laps and rock him because he couldn't sleep. He would sit

on my lap and watch the constellations. He was an extremely intelligent boy. He would watch these constellations and at about four or four thirty in the morning he would tell me, 'That group of stars will go about two inches farther and then there will be light and we can both go to sleep.' We spent night after night like that.

Ajit died in 1990 when my wife and I were in Seattle for a series of talks. He had taken a job and had to give it up because of the asthma. So he was at home his last years. He used to sit in his room and listen to the talks that were going on. He was extremely intelligent and had a very, very good understanding. I remember once a really ripe visitor came and we were talking. Ajit was listening. He went into the kitchen and told my wife, 'This one is a good one.' Ultimately, because the asthma kept him awake, he found that the only thing that would give him two or three hours sleep at night was alcohol. So he became an alcohol addict. Everyone warned him, 'Look, this is going to kill you.' And he said, 'I know more than that. I know all there is to know. Because I have to sleep, I have to drink.' And of course he continued. He got a liver disease and he died. It happened when I was in Seattle. A telephone call came that Ajit was extremely sick. My wife returned home and I continued with the talks. When she was in New York, on her way home, she called me. I had had a call that he had died, but I didn't tell my wife. Why make her grieve earlier?

❋ ❋ ❋

I have had my share of grief. My married daughter had a problem. The problem was her husband's drinking. Another problem was her husband's generosity; he was generous to a fault. So she had lots of problems. So that's why I say, 'I've had my share of grief. I have had my share of pain.'

※ ※ ※

Some years ago, two or three years ago, I had a back pain which the doctor really couldn't understand. Low back pain. I could sit and talk, so the back pain didn't stop the talks. The talks went on. I could sit, I could stand, and I could walk about, because a reasonable amount of pain was accepted. But I could not lie down. The doctor said, 'This is the first case I've found where you are not able to lie down. Usually there is relief from that pain in lying down.' So I spent quite a few days sitting in a chair.

So it is not that after Self-realization life becomes smooth. It does in the sense that you accept the pain and the pleasure. To that extent there is relief. But the grief and the pain which are part of your destiny are not wiped out.

Ramesh says that Self-realization is Acceptance. There is the understanding that whatever is happening, there is not someone doing it. 'So, if someone does something to hurt me. The hurt will happen. And even the happening of the hurt will depend on the extent of which "I" succumb to it. But there is never any feeling that someone has hurt me. So there is no feeling of hatred toward anyone. This is the peace I am talking about':

> At Maharaj's, in one particular case, someone asked a question — someone who had been coming for six months or six years or whatever. He asked a question. Maharaj got very angry. He said, 'You have been coming here all these years or months and you asked that silly question?' Anger arose. But literally the next

second, the same man suddenly realized what had happened and gave a very funny answer. And Maharaj's laugh was the loudest. Anger arose and then anger gave way to this laughter. The anger didn't sizzle in horizontal time. Maharaj didn't think, 'He is the man who made me angry. I will not laugh at his joke!' He didn't think that. His laugh was the loudest!

Ramesh says that just as there is no fear of life, there is no fear of death:

> When I was in Hawaii, we went on a helicopter ride. The pilot was a mischievous man. He would take us close to the waterfall, as if he were going to crash, and then turn right. Then he would turn back and look at the passengers. He saw that my wife was afraid that he was going to crash. But he said to me, 'On your face there was almost an expression of ecstasy.' It's because I felt cheated when we didn't crash. I've often thought that death must be a truly wonderful experience. One might say there is lurking a wish for death to get liberated from this body. Then I came across Ramana Maharshi's book in which he says exactly this: 'The sage not only is not afraid of death, but sometimes longs for it.'

※ ※ ※

My earlier guru had a small ashram where disciples could gather. One Saturday morning I happened to be there. Close by the ashram were a number of huts where the poorest of the poor lived with their children. The children, being children, were noisy, and they were playing on the streets. Suddenly there was a cry from somebody who was hurt. A couple of people were sent from the ashram to see what had happened. They brought in an old man who was hurt. He used to be an irregular visitor to the ashram. This man had Total Understanding. Self-realization had happened. He was such a simple man, and he was not concerned with the world recognizing him as Self-realized, so he really didn't give a damn.

This man went wherever God took him. He used to dress shabbily, never cared for his appearance, so he was a prime target for the playful children. Someone made fun of him and expected him to get angry. But he didn't get angry; he joined in the fun. He laughed himself, which irritated the boy who had made fun of him. So the boy threw a stone at him. And others started throwing stones, and he was injured.

So the two people from the ashram went out and they brought the old man in. People grumbled, 'This goes on all the time. The police won't do anything. Somebody should do something about it.' The old man wasn't injured badly. People cleaned up the wounds, applied something, and he was all right. While this was going on the old man said, 'What is all this grumbling about? I don't understand. What has really happened is that some hands threw stones at me and injured me; some other hands have cleaned up the wounds. What is all the fuss about?' It was not a statement made to impress anyone. It came straight from the heart.

❋ ❋ ❋

J. Krishnamurti's book, *The Awakening of Intelligence* had a tremendous impact on me at the appropriate time. I'm forever grateful to him for that impact. And yet, when I read in one of his books this passage, 'I never have dreams in the night', I closed the book.

I thought, 'Surely, a person who lives in the Himalayas never coming into contact with anything, that I can imagine. But he lives in Ojai or he lives in Zurich, he meets people, he gets angry when a question "how?" is asked.' So I was delighted when I came across a statement in a book about Ramana Maharshi. Someone asked him, 'Do you see dead people?' And Ramana Maharshi said, 'Only in my dreams.'

PERSONAL STORIES ABOUT RAMESH

The earliest inspiration in my life was Ramana Maharshi. I came across a book of his when I was twelve years old, and it made a tremendous impression. But it was not the destiny of this body-mind organism to sit at Ramana Maharshi's feet — although I could have done it because I was thirty-three years old when Ramana died. I could have gone, I wanted to, but I was so busy with my early career that it was not possible. So I could only take it that the destiny of this body-mind organism was not to be able to sit at Ramana Maharshi's feet, but at Nisargadatta's feet. Someone once asked Nisargadatta, 'Is there any difference between you and Ramana Maharshi?' And Nisargadatta, with his usual sense of humor, said, 'None at all, except that I'm slightly better dressed.'

The next two stories are about Ramesh's time working for the Bank of India:

> When I was working in a bank, most of my life and activities were concerned with the bank — being entertained and entertaining. So, wherever I was, wherever I went, I had to think in terms of a senior bank official being seen and heard. Once I retired, the privilege of anonymity was enormous!
>
> Once I was returning from Maharajs place. It was raining and the roads were muddy. I was walking along with a friend of mine with an umbrella, getting wet. It

just struck me then, 'If someone were to see me...' And just then I saw someone from the bank coming from the other direction. It was quite funny. He came. He passed by again. Then he muttered, 'No, it can't be.' And he walked away. It was extremely amusing.

So the privilege of anonymity is something you appreciate only when you are in a position to enjoy it. Earlier, if I went to a concert, I had to be seen. So I had to take a particular place, and if that concert made me sleepy, it was a very difficult situation. But later when I retired I could go and sit anywhere in the back and enjoy the concert.

❋ ❋ ❋

In my own case, at least from the age of twelve, perhaps earlier, two things were absolute convictions. One was that all this is absolutely unreal, and secondly, for me to have free will is utterly ridiculous. With these firm convictions this body-mind organism was not particularly suited for life in the world; and yet life in the world was terribly easy.

My father provided my higher education in England. I came back and got into a fairly good job, though at the lowest level. I am probably the first person in the Bank of India who started as a clerk and ended up as president. I had the deepest understanding that all this was just happening to me. There were other people more intelligent than I, working harder than I, but things seemed to come to me on a platter. So actually I had a feeling of guilt that things were happening to me without my effort; but they were happening and that was it. In a way there was quite a lot of envy and jealousy. And yet there was something inherent that did get appreciated by my superiors.

I had no training in advertisement. At a certain point the chairman, who was a real go-ahead person, decided that the Bank of India would advertise. There was no department for publicity or advertisement. So he said, 'All right, we'll get a hold of somebody.' Then certain people said, 'This is our chance. Let's see if we can get Balsekar now.' The advertising job was loaded onto me. At that time I had a very full day. I got a hold of certain advertising agencies, the leading ones, and I had a talk with them. And I knew they really didn't have any fresh ideas. I came to the conclusion that anyway, it was my head on the block, so I thought I'd see what I could do myself.

I got hold of a one-man agency, and a commercial artist and a photographer that this agency used. I worked on this advertising job at the end of the day when I'd had my dinner and came out and sat on my veranda open to the skies. And I really did not think. Things just kept happening for me in such a way that it was really a marvel to me, a miracle. At the end of the tired day, a tired mind just sat in that chair with what Krishnamurti calls 'awakened mind'. He says that awakened mind is not an idiot's mind; the awakened mind is the most alert mind. When I sat there without trying to concoct a policy or a plan, it was amazing how things came in.

The long and short of it is that the advertising that the Bank of India turned out was aggressive and effective. There was another bank whose head was in competition with our bank. This head of the other bank brought the top man of his advertising agency and said, 'Look. I'll give you two months. And if your advertising campaign for my bank is not at least as good as Bank of India's, you're out.' After two months, he was out! The Bank of India stayed ahead because the Bank of India's advertising was not run by a mind, it was run by Consciousness. A totally unequal struggle!

Ramesh talks about meeting Maharaj:

> Before I went to Nisargadatta Maharaj I had another guru for twenty years. He talked of non-duality, but his level of operating in this world stopped at the level of understanding of his guru. As far as he was concerned, his guru was directing all his actions. He was perfectly sincere and genuine, and he considered that his role was to help his disciples in all walks of life — material and spiritual. But from my point of view that was not what I needed. So again, as was natural to this organism, I didn't break off from him. I continued for twenty years, but I was aware that I needed something else. When I went to Maharaj, the very first day, the very first talk, I knew this was it. Those twenty years were not wasted. Those twenty years were part of the necessary process. Those twenty years made me understand what was not needed so that they also told me what was needed. So when what was needed came along I could recognize it straight away.

❋ ❋ ❋

Jean Dunn had written a couple of books on Nisargadatta's teachings. She wrote an article about Maharaj and the book *I Am That* in an issue of the *Mountain Path*, which is the official journal of the Ramanasramam, of which I think I've been a founder subscriber of twenty-five years. In that article about Nisargadatta Maharaj were a number of quotations from *I Am That*. So I got a copy immediately. At that time it was printed in two volumes. I read them over the weekend and went to Maharaj on Monday morning.

When I first climbed up the steps to his attic room there was no one else there except his personal attendant. Maharaj sat there as I climbed up the stairs and knelt before him. His first words were, 'You have come at last, have you? Come and sit down.' I thought he had probably addressed those words to someone else coming behind me so I looked back and there was no one else. But what was more interesting to me was that I had the distinct feeling that he was not aware that he had spoken those words. So his first words were a tremendous inspiration.

I had been in Bombay all my life, I'd been interested in this subject all my life, and yet I had not heard of Nisagardatta Maharaj until I read that article. So I mentioned it to someone else who started coming to Maharaj just about the time I did. I said, 'Here I was living in the same city, interested in the subject, and I had never come across Maharaj.' So he laughed. He said, 'At least you were some two or three miles away.' This man said he had lived for twenty years, five minutes walking distance from Maharaj, and he hadn't known about him. He used to buy books every year, quite a substantial sum, from a particular bookshop. He said he went to the bookshop one day and the salesman said, 'You'll probably be interested in this book,' and he gave him a copy of *I Am That*. He said, 'I took it home, read it, and here I am.' So, that's how things *happen*.

One year after meeting Nisargadatta Maharaj, the experience of Awakening happened for Ramesh:

> I have had two absolute convictions ever since I was a child. The first is that all this that appears real is not real. It is a sort of dream; it's an illusion. The corollary of that is, there is nothing I can do to change what is going to happen to me in anything — health, wealth, career, knowledge, whatever. These two were such convictions that the transformation was really very smooth. It was a sudden occurrence, and I know the time that it happened. It was during Deepavali, the Festival of Lights. On that occasion it was customary for Maharaj not to have a talk, and to have his place cleaned out. I started going to him in 1978, and this happened in 1979, almost exactly a year later. My friend suggested, 'Why stop the talk? Most people know where my address is. I can bring a map. Why don't we have it there?' Maharaj agreed.
>
> At that time the translations of Maharaj's talks into English were either done by me or someone else. That particular day the man who would have translated asked me to do so, and I said yes. As I started translating, it was a very peculiar situation. Normally the intellectual process was that I heard what he said, then there was an imbibing of what he said, and then the translating, and then the vocalizing of this understanding. But at that particular moment everything became One — Maharaj's talking was as if it were being echoed in English. I found myself hardly waiting for him to stop. It was as if I said, 'Why don't you stop. I know what you are saying.' It was so spontaneous that I could hardly hear his voice. It was as if it were coming from a distance. There was no waiting for him

to stop and for me to start. And it was noticed.

Maharaj didn't know English, and sometimes when he had doubts about the translation he would say, 'What did you say?' Very often I would have to say, 'Maharaj, I don't remember. I don't know. But if you want to know, there is the tape.' But after that day, not once did he ask me what it was I said. After that talk was over, my friend said, 'You were in great form today.' So I said, 'In what way?' He said, 'You were talking with an authority as if you didn't care if what you said was right or wrong or anything. Your voice was stronger, more authoritative, and you made more gestures than you usually do.' I didn't say anything. That was when It happened.

Another time Ramesh spoke in more detail about the actual moment of Awakening.

> There was impatience. The impatience was that I knew what it was all about. That Maharaj and I were not two different beings. There was a tremendous sense of oneness — not only between Maharaj and me, but in the existence of the Totality, a tremendous sense of oneness. Quite frankly, it seemed that the words were so unnecessary. There was a certain amount of impatience to get it over with. But it was a job being done. The feeling was, 'All this is unnecessary.' (I had a reluctant wish that someone else would translate, and then I wouldn't have to do the translation.) There was a sense of oneness, not something being translated. A tremendous sense of oneness. I repeat, oneness not only with myself and Maharaj, but oneness with the Totality.

In response to the question about how Maharaj acknowledged Ramesh's awakening, Ramesh says:

> The actual form was that he stopped asking me, from that day, to repeat what I said. He accepted that the interpretation or the translation would be spontaneous. But once he did say, and I don't like to say it very openly because what he said was, 'I am glad this has happened in at least one case.' I was so surprised, I looked at him. He said, 'Maybe, maybe in two or three other cases — a big maybe.' So that was the certification which came.

'When the understanding reaches a certain depth, and if the intention is for that particular body-mind organism to provide the teaching, then that Power – call it Consciousness or God – sends some people to that particular body-mind organism. How it happens is a mystery':

> Those who knew me earlier know that I am not a talker. If there is a group of eight or ten people, I am the listener. I've never been inclined to talk. But on this subject, I do talk. When I used to go to Maharaj's, one of his earliest instructions to all translators was that nobody talks about the subject except in his presence. He made it perfectly clear, probably because he was afraid of the teachings being misunderstood, and then misinterpreted. Later on he found that there was a fairly good understanding, as far as I was concerned.
>
> One particular morning when he was quite ill (he couldn't sit; he used to lie down) a group of about eight or ten people from about two hundred miles away came on a Sunday morning. His first instructions were, 'Please don't ask questions merely for the sake

of asking questions. I would like as few questions as possible. I am not in good health.' So between themselves they decided on which questions to ask and they started asking questions.

At a certain point Maharaj wanted to go downstairs from his loft (probably wanted to go to the toilet or whatever). Before he left, for the first time that I knew, he told these people, 'Don't stop asking questions. Continue to ask questions,' and pointing to me he said, 'He's authorized to talk.' But there were no questions, so there were no answers. Someone next to me said, 'Maharaj asked you to talk. If you don't talk, when he comes back he'll be angry.' So Maharaj came back and said, 'What's going on?' I said, 'Nothing. There were no questions so there were no answers.' He grumbled a little bit and the talks continued. This was only about a month before he died.

Maharaj knew that in spite of that authorization, I didn't talk. He knew it. Two days before he died he was very ill. He was so ill that his attendant had to bend down and put his ear close to his mouth if Maharaj wanted him to do something. Then suddenly he sat up with a tremendous burst of energy. He sat up on his elbow and looked at me, I was close by, and he said, 'Why don't you talk?!' And then he fell back. I thought that was the end, but it wasn't. He lasted for another twenty-four hours.

Earlier when he asked me, 'Why don't you talk?' it was because he knew I was not talking and as far as he was concerned he had given me the authorization to talk. But I wasn't talking because I didn't take it as a blanket authorization. That authorization was for a specific morning on a specific occasion. If Maharaj hadn't given that authorization, I don't know whether

I would have talked or not. Perhaps I would have, perhaps I would not have. I don't know. Anyway, from that moment on whenever people came to me, I did talk. One of them was Henry Dennison, and another individual was Heiner Siegelmann.

The real talking began when an Australian medical student from one of the nearby ashrams came to me and wanted to talk. So we talked for about an hour, or an hour and a half. He had been in India for about six months and he had taken a leave of absence from his studies, and he was to go back the next week. Before he left he asked if he could come back again. I said yes. So the next day he telephoned from somewhere on his way and said, 'Could I bring two or three other people?' So I said, 'Yes.' Among those three other people he brought was Ed Nathanson. After that, somehow, the number of persons continued to grow.

One of the people that came with Ed was an ashram swami in ochre robes. He listened, but I could see he was extremely restless. At the end of the talks he said he was very happy he came and he would like to come again. So he came two or three times. But all the time his conscience was obviously biting him that he should go to some other person to talk about the subject which was the main theme at the ashram. He was worried that Ed and another friend might expose him. So the swami literally hounded them out of the ashram. In a way, I think they were happy enough to leave by that time because of a change in the, let's say, management.

❋ ❋ ❋

One of the very first people to come and see me was an American called Henry Dennison. He wrote to me and said he was going around the world, he would be passing through Bombay, and could he come and see me for three or four days. So I said, 'Yes, of course.' So he came for three or four days and stayed for three months. All the time he was pressing me to go to Los Angeles where he would like to arrange some talks. In his words, many of his friends did not have both the time and the money to come to India and see me, but were deeply interested.

I was not interested in these talks; I was not interested in being known as a jnani. I was perfectly satisfied with life as it was going on, so I didn't show much interest. However, what Henry did during the last week before he left was to buy me a ticket by Air India Bombay, London, New York, Los Angeles, and back the same way. I had not even a passport. So of course when it reached that stage, then obviously Life wanted me to go to Los Angeles and I did. That is how the talks in America started.

The first year in Hollywood, 1987, the talks were in Henry Dennison's house. It was a beautiful house, situated on the edge of a lake — big enough to accommodate thirty or forty people. I just couldn't imagine that someone could live in a big house like that and not have a servant. To me it was unimaginable. Now I know many Americans live like that, except a few millionaires who have servants. So in the mornings, Henry would wake up and prepare breakfast for us.

While I was there, I got up fairly early, and there were several magazines. One of them was called *Yoga Journal*. It was quite popular, and what came to my attention while browsing through it were a number of advertisements, promising — I'm not sure if they used the word Enlightenment or not, but what was implied was 'Enlightenment over the weekend' for $350. Enroll before such and such a date. So I closed the magazine, sat there stupefied, and said to myself, 'What the hell am I doing in this place?' That was my reaction. And the answer came to me two or three days later after the talks started.

A man came to me, knocked on the door, about eight o'clock. The talks started at nine. His eyes were red; it was quite obvious that he had had a sleepless night. He came in, saw me standing, and he laid down at my feet full length as an Indian would do, touched my feet, and while he was there he said, 'I have not done this before any other person.' Then he got up and told me his story.

He had been a seeker for thirty-eight years. A personal friend of J. Krishnamurti, he had read everything that could be read. He said that he had received the flyer from Henry Dennison that I would be coming. This man said that when he looked at the photograph he thought, 'This is the end of my search.' And he wanted to talk to me. So he called Henry and said, 'I want to talk to Ramesh.' Henry said, 'He'll be talking here in three days. Why do you want to bother him now?' So he didn't.

But this man apparently needed just a little push, and he got that push, and he got the Final Understanding. I had no doubt about that after I talked to him for a little while. And then, when he went to the room at the talks and took his usual place, then it struck me that I had the answer to, 'What the hell am I doing here?' I was there for this person's needs. And if there was this person, maybe there would be others too.

By programming, I would rather walk than sit. So if there is nothing to be done I usually walk around the apartment from one corner of the apartment to the other corner. It takes me about twenty-five steps. I keep walking, assuming that twenty-five minutes with interruptions will make a mile. So I roughly calculate that I walk about four miles a day. What I noticed suddenly one day was that while I was walking my mantra was spontaneously happening. After walking for a while, being tired, I just laid down for five minutes. My wife saw me lying down for five minutes, then getting up as if I had something important to do. She said, 'You were lying down for only five minutes. Couldn't you take rest for twenty minutes?' So I said, 'I was not lying down to rest. I was lying down and the rest happened.' So when I lay down, singing will happen. My mantra is the Shiva mantra. It happens. All these years that is what is happening. Witnessing, nonwitnessing, and in the meanwhile the mantra goes on spontaneously. It was a very pleasant surprise for me to come across a sentence from Ramana Maharshi, 'When spontaneous japa [the repetition of the mantra] happens, it is Self-realization.'

In an informal interview, which occurred during one of the talks in Kovalam Beach, Ramesh was asked about changes in his relationship with others as a result of the Awakening:

I think in the relationship with others, the marked difference, which could perhaps be seen by others and, felt by others, is a far deeper sense of compassion and much, much less confrontation. It is always a feeling of compassion and never one of confrontation or any negative feeling.'

Ramesh is the author of many books. These books are written with a great deal of spontaneity. Ramesh talks about how the process of writing about the teachings began, and how it was part of the process of Awakening:

> When I was with Maharaj, at a certain moment actually it was in the middle of the night — I got up and felt the urge to write. I started writing and it turned out to be in the form of free verse. Poetry was one of my bugbears in school; I never did like poetry. Poetry was strange to me and yet the first writing that arose was in the form of free verse. I had it typed and I read it over to Maharaj and translated it and said, 'This has just come out.' So he suggested that I put it in print and have a few copies made. I thought I would distribute it free, but Maharaj was a businessman. He said, 'If you give something free, it will have no value. Put at least R5 on it.' So I had that done, and that is the brown booklet which is called, *The Whole Story*. That was as far back as 1979.
>
> When this writing comes, this does not mean total awakening. It still is an indication of the process of enlightenment. It is part of the process. During that process other things may happen. A sense of fear may arise. The body-mind organism could undergo certain changes — some violent and some not so violent — and some undergo no changes at all. So what happens in this is totally unimaginable, totally unpredictable. So seeking is a process in which anything can happen until the process is complete. When the process is complete there is no doubt about it; there is no question about it. What is real is very real, what is unreal is seen as unreal, and there is a great experience of the impersonal functioning of Totality.